One Thing
After Another

To Marge:
I'm so blessed to have
our friendship! God Richly
Bless You & Your Family!
Love You!

Rose

ROSE MARIE ARTHUR

ISBN 978-1-64191-212-9 (paperback)
ISBN 978-1-64191-213-6 (digital)

Christian Faith Publishing, Inc.
832 Park Avenue
Meadville, PA 16335
www.christianfaithpublishing.com

Precious Moments Small Hands Bible, New King James Version. Edited by Thomas Nelson. Nashville, Tennessee: Thomas Nelson Inc., 1982.

Printed in the United States of America

Contents

Acknowledgements

I want to thank, first and foremost, our dear Heavenly Father. I dedicate this book to Him. May all glory, honor and praise be His forever and ever.

For my parents, who are no longer here. I was so lucky to have you as my parents. You were the best parents in the world. I love and miss you both immensely.

I want to thank my daughter for helping me type the book and my other daughter for helping me express what I would like for the cover of the book. I would also like to thank my husband for the technical support and for all the other support given in this process. It would not have been possible without everyone's help and support. Thank you so much!

I want to thank Lisa Bolen, my literary agent, Shannon Vernier and Nicole Hepak, my publication specialists, and everyone at Christian Faith Publishing Company for all of your time and work in helping me make this book possible. I couldn't have done it without all of you.

For anyone who I have hurt throughout my lifetime, I am truly sorry. I hope peace, love, and joy for you all. I also forgive all of those who have trespassed against me.

I want everyone to know that what is written in this book is my story, feelings, and what has happened in my life, the good and the bad. It is only explaining what I have gone through with my life. This book is not intended to put anyone down. It is being written to help others who are suffering in any way, shape, or form. I pray that God will richly bless all of you. God's peace and love.

Prologue

In the Beginning

It was 1968. My mother was forty-two years old and my father was fifty-one. I had three older brothers age twenty, nineteen, and fifteen. The oldest brother was a truck driver and was married. His wife was expecting in November of that year.

My mother wasn't feeling very well after April 20, 1967. This was my father's birthday. She went to the doctor. He diagnosed her with a tumor. Then one day, the tumor had grown immensely. She went back to the doctor. The doctor looked her over again, realizing he had misdiagnosed her condition greatly. He had to break the news that it was not a tumor as thought of previously. It was a baby!

"You're pregnant," he said.

"Oh, boy! Now what do we do? Should we give the baby up for adoption? We are so old and won't even make it to see the child graduate," said my concerned father.

My grandfather convinced my father to just have the child and raise it, and so they did. January 21, 1968 arrived and so did the baby. It was a girl. They had wished for a girl since they already had three boys. My mother wanted a girl because her mother and sister had long hair, and they always took turns combing each other's hair. She longed to be able to brush and comb her little girl's hair.

The grandparents on my father's side only had grandsons, so a granddaughter was a welcomed sight. The grandparents on my mother's side were equally excited even though they had a large number of grandchildren. This was going to be the youngest grandchild. Being the only girl and the youngest in the family, no matter where this little girl was, she was smothered with unconditional love, born into this perfect little world. Well, that little girl was me. I became an aunt at nine months old, and this is my story.

Chapter 1

A Piece of Heaven on Earth

I was definitely a free-spirited barefoot little country girl, which you could say was a tomboy. I grew up in the country outside a little town in the Midwest. There were rolling hills with plenty of land to run free. A little creek that ran through the land divided the yard in the back from the fields. There was a bridge that you could cross over to get to the fields, and behind that were woods, a pond, and railroad tracks. This was the land that had been in the family since the 1800s.

My grandfather had a barn on his property. It caught on fire and burned down, so he rebuilt the big barn first and then built their home and all of their other barns on this land. It also included a shed, which was my grandfather's workshop, a chicken coop, and I can't forget the outhouse. It was a real live Farmville, like on Facebook on the computer now days.

My grandfather fell off the roof of his barn while building it and broke his neck. They told him he would be paralyzed for the rest of his life. However, he proved everyone wrong and walked again. The house was a two-story farmhouse with a cement basement. There was a huge wraparound front porch. The backdoor was the mudroom that went into the kitchen. They had an old-fashioned black water pump by the sink. You had to pump the handle by hand to bring the water up. They had a swinging door that led to the dining room. They would prop it open with an old-fashioned iron as a doorstop. It was made of real iron and was very heavy.

The bathroom was off the kitchen. You would walk down a hall past the dining room to enter the living room. There was a beautiful wooden staircase that led upstairs with a diamond window at the top to look out. There was also a back staircase that went to the bathroom from upstairs and both staircases met together to also lead to the basement stairs. My grandparent's bedroom was off the living room. They had lots of bedrooms upstairs.

My father bought some of my grandfather's land and built his home next to my grandfather's. There was even a sidewalk that went through our yard from our home to my grandmother and grandfather's home. I traveled up and down that sidewalk with my bike and pink wicker baby buggy over and over again. I had memorized every crack in that sidewalk so vividly, and it is still there today with every crack still the same. My father eventually bought even more land behind our home and put in a pond. He planted pine trees all around it. At the far end of the pond, he planted some pine bushes and crabapple trees that bloomed into beautiful light and dark pink blossoms in the springtime. He also planted a weeping willow tree at that end of the pond.

In the pond were bullfrogs that lined the outside of the pond. As you would walk by, they would jump into the water. They hung around until my father bought fish at a hatchery to put in the pond. He had bought catfish, bluegills, bass, and minnows. He would feed the fish with bread and fish pellets that looked like dog food. They were his babies. The catfish grew extremely large. He would also put copper sulfate in the water, and it turned the water to a bluish-greenish color. It looked so pretty up against the green grass. He had white stones around the edges of the pond.

The front of the pond was a sandy walk out beach that had boards under the water to let us know when we had reached the deep end. It would drop off from there. The deep end went down twenty feet. We had a raft, rowboat, and a dock as well. We had two really big weeping willow trees by the shallow end of the pond. A big white wooden shed stood in the middle of the two trees. The trees were great for shade. We would sit under them by the pond. They were also great for climbing. I built my own tree house. I used one board and two nails and climbed my way up the tree with the materials and a hammer and nailed the one board down between two branches. That was where I sat, on that one lonely board. It was the best tree house ever. I made it all by myself and I loved it.

One particular maple tree was my favorite to climb. We also had a big maple tree in the front yard in front of the house. My father had two big crabapple trees along the side of the house with some pine trees to block the wind and weather against the west of the house. Storms always came from that direction, going east from the west. The crabapple trees were pink and burgundy in the spring and were beautiful. My father had a true green thumb.

He planted all kinds of fruit trees as well. We had two pear trees and two apricot trees, but one died. He had two sweet cherry trees. One was yellow cherries and the other one was red cherries. He had a sour cherry tree, two peach trees, and an apple tree. The white blossoms in the spring were beautiful.

He didn't stop with the trees either. There was a red rose bush and three lilac bushes dividing my father and grandfather's land. Two were purple and one was white. The aroma was a wonderful fragrance as the breeze would carry the smell over the yard.

There were flowers of all kinds: yellow daffodils, pink and burgundy peonies along the white shed, tulips, lilies, and a beautiful yellow forsythia bush at the end of the driveway. My mother also planted petunias in all colors. They had a pussy willow bush as well. My mother would go across the road and gather bittersweet, which is orange-colored berries from the ditch, for fall decorations. It was by our mailbox.

My father also had his big garden. He would plant corn, tomatoes, cherry tomatoes, potatoes, onions, cucumbers, cabbage, carrots, lettuce, strawberries, and raspberries. There was this really large mulberry tree at my grandfather's that I would climb up in and eat until my heart's content with juice stains everywhere. There were also rhubarb plants. I would pick it and chomp on it as if it were a stalk of celery. Bitter, oh so bitter. There was a walnut tree back by the creek, and I would go back and gather nuts from the ground and sit there breaking them open to dig out the walnut and eat them. I also found milkweed back there one time and broke it open and rubbed the milk on a wart I had on my knee and it went away and never came back.

I was assigned jobs around the house as well. There were always fruit trees that had to be picked, grass to mow, sheds to paint, and I even had to crawl under the house in the creepy, muddy, spider-infested crawlspace to put insulation up with a staple gun.

The dandelions got in on the action too. My mother had me pick them, and she would cook them. Dandelion greens. Of course, I had to take time out to say "he loves me, he loves me not" with the petals and "mama had a baby and her head popped off" while popping the head of the dandelion off its stem. I blew the seeds from the dead ones around, and I would smear the yellow of the dandelion onto my skin as if I were painting myself.

My father and brother helped me plant my first tree. It was the little pine tree you get from first grade that was a little stick. Everyone usually runs over it with the lawn mower and it dies, but not my father with the green thumb. I would go and water it. I was so proud of it. It grew very tall. I had my picture taken next to it as we both grew. By my graduation from high school, it was taller than me. It is still there today and towers way above me.

Needless to say, springtime was absolutely beautiful there. The white, pink, burgundy, yellow, purple, light green, green grass, blue water and sky just filled your sense of sight to the utmost. My father had made his own piece of heaven here on earth.

Chapter 2

Home, Church, Sundays, and Neighbors: Those were the Days

Like I mentioned before, my father built our home. It was a ranch-style home, which is one story with just a crawl space for a basement. It was a three-bedroom home with one bath until he extended it and made a fourth bedroom and a half bath with it. There was an attached garage with the laundry room attached to the back of the garage. They called it the utility room. The furnace and electrical box were in there too. The garage then led out to the side patio. I remember the garage door was a very heavy wooden door and had to be lifted by hand until I bought an electrical garage door opener for my dad years later.

The living room and dining room were at the front of the house, and it was all one big room. The walls were made of plaster with an arch leading to the hall that led to the bedrooms and the bathroom in the back of the house. My parents' bedroom was in the front of the house. It was painted in the mint green color for a long time and then they changed it to more of a dark cream color.

The kitchen was located in the back of the house and was done in the very nostalgic '50s theme. Yellow-and-black counters and tiles on the walls matched the yellow with black flowers of the metal kitchen table and chairs. He custom-built all of the cupboards in a gingerbread house look. The bathroom was done in pink and black tiles on the walls. He built a corner rounded self that was built into the sink.

The patio eventually was all enclosed with windows and sliding glass doors. He put in a solar-powered heating system on our roof. He also poured cement in the backyard and made a basketball court. He also turned the stone driveway into a cement driveway. He even added a gas tank to be used to fill the vehicles when needed.

We went to a little white country church just down the road on the corner from us. It was a Methodist church. My great-grand-father helped build this church many years ago. It had a beautiful painting of Jesus walking up a hill carrying a sheep while other sheep surrounded him. I was baptized there. I grew up lighting the candles, getting to watch them pull the large rope that rang the church bell in the bell tower, and going to Sunday school.

When I was real young, they dressed me as an angel for a Christmas program. I was so shy and scared, I started to cry. I had to have my mother by my side at all times. If she wasn't next to me in Sunday school, I would run upstairs to try and find her. My Sunday school teacher was a teacher in another school district. I unfortunately didn't have her as my schoolteacher, but I did for my Sunday school and was richly blessed by this. She showed me so much love, and we have a special bond to this day.

The members of the church also showed me so much love. I remember the old-time religious hymns that we would sing and how the windows would be opened in the summer with the cross breeze blowing over us and looking out at the sun shining down on the fields beside us. I had felt so much joy and had never felt so close to the Lord and had felt so much love, peace, and security. I remember singing all the songs in Sunday school as well and going to Bible school.

My mother would fix a pot roast with potatoes and carrots and put it in the oven. When we got home from church, it was ready to eat and it made the whole house smell so good. My father would read the Sunday newspaper and give me the funnies. I would sneak up on him and bang on his newspaper while he was reading it. He would lower the paper and look over the top of it at me and would smile until I did it too much then he would look at me with that disappointed look in his eyes and I would stop because I hated to disappoint him. He would also watch sports on the television.

At other times, we would eat Swiss steak at a restaurant in another town about half an hour away. It was great to go there for lunch right after church on Sunday. We would also go into the next state over, because we lived close to the border of two other states, and we would drive around several lakes and admire the lake front properties.

Our neighbors were all great. We knew all our neighbors and we would visit all of them. We were always there for each other when someone needed a hand. My father had one sibling, a sister. She was a very special aunt. She lived on the next road over. It was a four-mile square, and she lived dead center to our home. I would ride my bike around the square. My first stop was the wild strawberry patch along the ditch. I would have to pick them and eat them right there on the spot. Then I would stop at the first neighbor to visit her. She baked cakes and would always share her extra frosting with me. Then I would leave and head off to my aunts. She made wonderful homemade sugar cookies and would always give me some to eat. My grandmother and great aunts would compete with each other at the fair, all with the same cookie recipe, and my one great aunt would win it every time. After eating my cookies, I would get back on my bike and head home.

I loved coasting down the hills. Going up them was another story. I would also ride my bike to a little town about a mile and half from where our home was. They had a little store with a mighty big candy counter. I would take my piggy bank and off I would go. They had little Tootsie Rolls for a penny or pieces of gum. They would give you a little brown bag, and I would very carefully choose my candy. I would drop it on the counter, and they would count it. I would pay them with my change from my piggy bank, take my little bag of candy, and head home on my bike. I eventually had an actual Tootsie Roll bank. I remember shaking it one time. The lid flew off and tootsie rolls flew everywhere, and I screamed, "It's tootsie rolling." My best friend was there with me in the living room when I did that, and we would just giggle and then later picked them all up.

I also would take my roller skates and skateboard down the road where there was this really cool curve on a hill. What fun! Those were the days!

Chapter 3

THIS IS MY FATHER

My father was a good Christian man who was friendly to everyone. He had a gentle spirit with lots of patience. He was very committed. He always had a smile on his face, and he was an honest man. He rarely got upset, unless a favorite team was losing, something didn't go right while working on a project, or something in politics. He was never upset with anyone. It was usually only the situation that would upset him if things weren't going well.

My father knew how to go to the top to get answers and solve problems. He didn't like to travel very far distances, and he didn't like crowds of people. He didn't like to wait in long lines or hotel rooms. He was good at handling money. He took care of all the finances in the home and did all the driving. He drove a white-and-light-green pickup truck. I remember riding in it with the windows down and the wind blowing in my hair, thinking I was so cool. Eventually, my father bought a used Lincoln. That was his baby, his real pride and joy.

My father was a fix-it man. He loved to build things. He watched baseball on the television. He always listened to polka music on the radio. We even went to a small town for a polka fest one time. It was kind of fun. He loved to watch *Hee Haw* and *Lawrence Welk*. I remember this was always on the television on Saturday evenings, and I would try and escape by taking a bubble bath with Mr. Bubbles. He would watch Billy Graham when he came on TV as well.

He loved to chase down fire trucks or police to see what was happening in the neighborhood. I remember hopping in the car in my pajamas on the spur of the moment to go check it out with him.

He eventually bought a scanner to keep him informed on everything. My father never smoked, but he did try chewing tobacco when he was young one time and it made him sick and he never did it again. He wasn't a drinker of alcohol, but he did have a wine bottle in the refrigerator and would take a swig of it from time to time for a belly-ache. He played the trumpet when he was younger, and he bowled a perfect three hundred game one time.

He graduated from high school. Their class was small, maybe ten students. Three of them were cousins, my father and two other students. My father's class reunions meant a lot to him, and he wouldn't miss any of them, as well as any of his former classmates. They were one of the oldest classes that were all still living and who all would still attend the reunions, something to celebrate. There was an idea in the works for them to go to Chicago to be on the *Oprah Winfrey Show*. That never transpired. My father's dear friend in his class was also his neighbor, and they were close their whole life. What is really neat is that his friend had three daughters and I became really close to the one daughter. We have remained close all these years as well.

He had my grandfather, his father, live with us when he got older for six months at a time. Then my grandfather would stay with my aunt the other six months, until eventually he was put in a nursing home. My grandmother died when I was two years old. While staying with us, my grandfather was in a wheelchair. Someone drove over his mailbox, and he was determined to roll his wheelchair over to his shed to bang out the dents in his metal mailbox with a hammer. He would go through the yard and fall out of his chair. He always wore green jean bib overalls.

My grandfather was a farmer and a carpenter. He always put his thumb between his first finger and middle finger. I don't know why I remember this, but I do. He eventually had to sell his property. I remember seeing him sitting in his wheelchair on his front porch, watching the whole thing happen, with tears rolling down his face. There were a lot of arrowheads for sale he found on the land. He was in a nursing home at this time and always checked each day off on his calendar. It was not long after the sale of his home when he died.

The calendar's days were crossed off lighter and lighter until his last. His watch stopped when he died.

For years, my father was a farmer and a carpenter like my grandfather. Then before I came around, he became a salesman. He sold grease and oil in his territory. This was the profession he was in when I was born and throughout my childhood. He would take me, my mom, and my brother on the road when he would go selling. We would wait patiently in the car until he was done and then we would always go out to a restaurant to eat lunch.

One time, he was selling to a factory. They had railroad tracks there. A train was stopped, and the engineer let me ride through the town with him in the front where he sat to drive the train. I got to pull the whistle at the intersection. How fun! We would go to the mall in that town a lot, too.

My mother was a housewife and had never drove before, so my mother liked going along to get out of the house. I remember how my mother would bring the potty chair along, and that is how I became potty trained. I would go, and they would dump it out. It worked out well. When we would get home, my dad would sit down at his desk and finish filling out the orders to be mailed in. The UPS man would deliver the boxes of oil to our home for my father to deliver.

We had the big black dial desk phone with the cord and a party line. You would have to share the telephone lines with other neighbors. You may pick up the phone to make a call and the neighbors would be on talking and you would have to wait until they hung up to use the phone. We also dialed zero to get an operator for any kind of phone assistance or an emergency. That doesn't exist anymore. Now you dial 911. I remember putting my finger in the hole of the number I wanted and turning it until it reached the metal stopper with each number until you made your call. If you didn't reach the stopper all the way with a number, you would have to hang up and start all over again. As a kid, I thought it was cool to call time and temperature. You could also call dial a prayer. My father would use the phone a lot to call on customers. My father did really well in his business. This is my father.

Chapter 4

THIS IS MY MOTHER

My mother grew up in a very religious family of Mennonites on her mother's side of the family. Although she didn't always go by the Mennonite's rules, she was a God-fearing Christian. She did have a fear, a fear of bats, and for good reason. She had a couple run-ins with them. In my parent's first house, which was made of brick, they would get in the upstairs bedroom. My father would chase them with a broom in his long underwear. Another time, while she was at church outside in the evening, they flew down from the bell tower and landed in her hair. It got tangled up, but finally they got it out. That was enough for her.

I think my mother was afraid of running out of time. She was always in a hurry, in a hurry to get somewhere and in a hurry to leave. She would have to be at church an hour before it started. We would be the first ones there and would have to wait in the parking lot until someone with a key showed up to let us in. As soon as church was over, we had to be the first to leave. Lunch had to be at ten o'clock in the morning and supper at three o'clock in the afternoon.

The older my mother got, the harder it was for her to hear. I would have to ask her to repeat something that may be important to me to make sure she heard it correctly. I always felt I was screaming so she could hear me. She loved to talk on the phone but only for a short while. She would think of something she wanted to say, call you up and say it, and then she was ready to hang up. Then she would think of something else and call you back again and could do that all day if you let her. She was always done with the conversation and would hang up when she would say, "Okay!" It didn't matter if you were still talking or not and had more to say. You would have to call her back or wait for her to call you right back. Oh my mother, what a hoot! Like my father, she never smoke or drank but she did down a beer one time at my high school graduation party. It was really funny.

There were so many nights my mother couldn't sleep. We could hear her moving about in the kitchen baking pies. It wouldn't take long for the aroma to hit our bedrooms to know they were either apple or cherry. She also made the best baked apples ever. During the day, she would have her apron or housedress on. She would put the ironing board up between the kitchen and dining room doorway and iron.

My mother also had an artistic side to her. She could draw really well. When I became a little older, she made things for me on the sewing machine. She made clothes for my Barbie and made me animal pillows. She made some neat blankets, too, all of which I still have. We would do crafts together. We painted by number, made hot pads, put puzzles together, and made hook rugs. My mother also liked taking pictures and had a little brownie camera. She had lots of photo albums that I would look through often. I still have those as well.

When we would go to pot lucks, my mother would make baked beans and put them in a Styrofoam cooler, and the smell was fantastic. When we would have company over that we would cook for, she would go to the coat closet and get the extra leaf to the dining room table out to put it in the table to make it larger. This was always exciting to me, because I knew company was coming and it was always a big deal.

In my parent's room, my mother had a wooden vanity set with a matching chair. There were drawers on both sides and a drawer in the middle that pulled out. You could slide the chair under the middle drawer. The top was flat with a huge circle mirror. I loved this vanity and wish I had it today. I would play with my mother's jewelry, usually beaded necklaces. She also had a box of handkerchiefs. I would go through them.

She would have a couple different ladies do her hair for her. My mother called them in curls. Today's terminology would be a perm. I would sometimes go with her. In the third grade, I got brave and had an in curl/perm. It turned out awful. My school picture was taken with it. After my mother would get her in curl, she would wear a headscarf to protect it if she went anywhere. She would also put pink plastic curlers in her hair at night, put a hair net over it, and sleep that way. She would take them out in the morning. I tried that a couple of times. It is not a very comfortable way to sleep. Maybe that is why she was up all night baking pies.

She had a fake fur my father got her. I have that and her pink wedding dress. My parents were married around the Depression and World War II era. You couldn't find any white wedding dresses. My mother's veil was really long. I don't have that though. Some other things I have that were passed down through the years that mean a lot to me are my grandmother's, on my father's side, gold bracelet she wore on her wedding day, the wooden rocking chair that was in her kitchen and is in mine today, and her quilt that has pieces of her wedding dress in it. I also have my great-grandmother's, on my mother's side, white wicker flower basket. It goes well on my front porch with the white railings.

My grandfather on my mother's side adored me, and I adored him. I would run into the house and go straight to the living room to his favorite chair and hop on his lap. My grandmother always sat in her chair next to my grandfather in the corner. She hardly ever said two words. My aunt lived there, too. She would sit next to my grandmother in a hard-backed chair. She would always say to me, "Bless your little heart."

They were Mennonites on my grandmother's side, and the women wore their hair really long and put it up with a prayer hat on to cover it. It was a really long process. They would brush each other's hair because it was so long. Then they would braid it and then wrap the braids around and around until it all fit on their heads and then they put the prayer hat on, which looked like a white net.

My grandparents lived in a town about a half hour away. That is where my mother grew up. They had a barn, and there were railroad tracks behind them. They had an apple orchard and a lot of grape vines. They also had a big garden. They would make cider and apple butter. They sold the cider and apples.

They had a huge enclosed back porch that led down to the basement. It was off the kitchen. My grandparent's bedroom was off the kitchen. The dining room went off the kitchen on the other side, and my aunt's bedroom came off from the dining room. The living room went off from the other part of the kitchen, and the bathroom was off the living room. They had an upstairs that had another kitchen and bedrooms that could have other people live up there if they wanted to. They did not have a television.

My parents and grandparents on both sides were not materialistic. When Christmas and birthdays came around, I didn't receive anything, and I didn't expect to. That was just something we never did. My grandparents had a bowl that had sat on the back porch. It was a plastic bowl that had Peter Rabbit with his mother on it. I loved that bowl and would always play with it. One time I asked if I could have it and they gave it to me. I still have it. It was the only thing I got, and I cherish it. My grandfather would give me circus peanuts. It was a type of candy. They were the orange marshmallows that looked like peanuts. They were always in the corner kitchen cupboard. My grandfather wore jeans that were ripped and torn and would not get rid of them. He was comfortable in them. My grandmother always wore a plain dress with an apron.

My mother had two sisters and three brothers. Her three brothers were all ministers. My grandparents, mom, and her siblings all attended the Church of the Brethren through her childhood. My mother and one of her sisters cut their hair short. They were the rebels of the family, since this was against the Mennonite's rules. This is my mother.

Chapter 5

THESE ARE MY BROTHERS

I had three older brothers who were almost old enough to be my fathers. They all graduated from high school. My oldest brother was a truck driver, married, and had two girls and two boys. I never really knew him very well since he was already moved out before I was born and always gone on the semi. My second brother always lived at home with our parents. He never was married or had any children. The youngest brother married, had a son, divorced, and went into the army.

He was stationed at Fort Knox, Kentucky. He then went to Germany to guard the Berlin Wall. I remember taking a trip to Fort Knox with my family to go see him. My niece and I had our picture taken with him in his uniform. One summer, before he divorced and went into the army, he and his wife visited us at our home. They brought a Siamese cat with them, and we had to take care of it for a few days. I was supposed to go to Bible school and I didn't want to leave because they were there.

My brother was so cool with his bright-orange-and-purple bell-bottomed pants on, playing his eight-track tapes, washing his jacked-up blue sports car, and eating bacon, lettuce, and tomato sandwiches or egg sandwiches. I thought he was just it. His wife also had a shirt and pants on with strawberries on it, and I loved it. While I was watching the cat, it would climb the curtains, jump on my head, and attack me. I thought this was odd since we lived in the country and would acquire a lot of outdoor cats and none of them would do that to me. I was scared of that thing and haven't had much luck with Siamese cats since. My mother kept it in the laundry room because I was so scared of it.

When my brother returned from the army, we had to go pick him up at the airport. It was storming, a very unusual storm. It was snowing with thunder and lightning at night. We got lost and finally got home very early the next morning. He wanted to go see our aunt and decided to walk over. We drove to get him and take him the rest of the way but he beat us. We got stuck in the snow a half mile away. We all got out and walked the rest of the way in the very, very cold blowing snow and wind. I was too small to walk through the drifts, so my brother carried me. I remember being so cold and didn't think we would ever get there. We finally got into my aunt's yard, and my brother dropped me into the snow bank, and I started to cry. Finally, my father picked me up and carried me the rest of the way into the house. My aunt had us take our wet clothes off and wrapped us in blankets, and we stayed a few nights until we were all dug out.

My brother, after the army, also gave me my first dog. He was a white beagle with big brown circles on him. I named him Sockie. At this same time, my oldest brother divorced while my youngest brother remarried and had a daughter and started taking care of his son from his first marriage. My oldest brother then remarried, and she had two daughters from her first marriage. They came to live on my parent's land. They had plumbing, sewage, water, and electricity all hooked up to a house trailer behind our home. They also put up a little wooden brown shed.

Before my oldest brother remarried, he would come home off the semi from time to time. My mother would get so excited when he would come home and get the coffee pot going and the cookies out. A new drink mix came out at that time called Tang. It was a powder you mix with water and it was an orange flavor. It was what the astronauts drank while in space. We would drink that too when my brother came home. We would drink it hot or cold either one. My mother always had ice cream sandwiches on hand and 3 Musketeers for when company came to give them. I was always excited too since I didn't know him very well. I thought this might be a good opportunity to get to know him better. These are my brothers.

Chapter 6

GROWING UP

Now, to introduce you to me, as a small child, I was a very shy and scared child. If you were not my parents or grandparents, forget it. I would not have anything to do with you. I did not like strangers or to be held by them. I was terrified. I especially did not like people in costumes where I could not see their true identity. Santa Claus and clowns were extremely frightening to me.

Our church had a float one year in the Fourth of July parade. My mother, father, and I rode on the float. I remember there was a clown walking back and forth with all the people, and I prayed he would not see me or come near me. I wanted to hide under my mom and dad so bad. Fortunately, I survived the parade and all was fine.

As I grew a little older, I did reach out and became friends with my neighbor across the street. She was the same age I was. She became my first best friend that I had. We would play with our Barbie dolls and we would play dress up. She had two sisters and two brothers. The brothers liked to pick on me as boys do to girls that age. One liked to pick on me more than the other. They would pick me up and try to hold me upside down and lower my face into the toilet bowl. I absolutely hated that and would be so upset and scared. Then one time they made snowballs with stones in them and threw them at me. It hurt so badly. I would go back home crying. I would say something to the parent, but every time I tried to say anything, I was accused of being a tattletale. I was being bullied. My parents advised me to just stay away or just have my friend come to our house. I felt they were so mean to me.

Till this day, I still hate the word *tattletale*. It was used too liberally. I could see if you were a gossip or a troublemaker, then okay. That is a tattletale to me, but when you are being picked on and bullied, asking for help and not keeping secrets and lying about it is not considered tattling. There is a big difference there. This was my first experience with learning there are mean people out there. I remember always wanting to be very close to my parents so they could protect me. Somehow, at a very young age, I was frightful. I was frightful I would lose my parents, my safety net, my protection, and unconditional love.

As I grew, it was time for me to start kindergarten. I remember the summer I was five and my parents bought me school supplies and a lunch box. I loved my lunch box so much. It was metal, and there was a red flannel pattern on it.

Since we lived in the country, I had to take the bus to school. That was where all of my fears became full force to the surface again. I was scared to death. My mom would stand at the end of the drive with me and wait for the bus. When the bus arrived, she walked me across the road and encouraged me to climb the steps to get on. Slowly and eventually, with the help of my best friend across the street, I got on the bus without my mom.

I got through the first couple of years of school okay with the help of my best friend. Then tragedy took place. My best friend's father died from a brain tumor and the family had to move. What was I going to do now? She was my security blanket! However, second grade started anyways without her and I developed another wonderful friendship for many years to come with a new person.

As I just lost my one and only best friend, a new girl moved to our school and we bonded immediately. We rode the same bus, were in the same grade, with the same teacher and classroom. We became such good friends that she would come to my house and I would go to hers. She quickly became the sister I never had. We would sit on the bus together and do the handclaps to songs as well as kitty whiskers and cat's cradle with string. We did a lot of pretending. We played restaurant, secretary, and sometimes school too. We built tents inside with the dining room table, chairs, and blankets. We would have sleepovers and sleep in our sleeping bags in our tents that we made.

We played with our Barbies and our stuffed animals. She had a pink kitty named Cali, and I had a yellow teddy bear named Fluffy. When I was younger, I had a white puppy I carried everywhere and loved it. I don't know whatever happened to it. She also had a big dog named Henry. We would dress them up, and they were our babies.

We would also ride our bikes and pretend they were our cars. The patio was wide open with rod iron posts, and we would ride our bikes right through the patio pretending it was the gas station, and the rod iron posts were the gas pumps. We had a doghouse that was where the "laundromat" was. The doghouse was the washer and then the dryer.

I had a record player with records, and we would listen and sing to the music. I have always loved singing. We would play 'Name that Tune.' One would hum or sing a few words, while the other guessed the title of the song. We would use my albums as menus when we played restaurant. I had a disco album that had the song Fifth of Beethoven on it. I would say that was five pieces of bacon for my menu. What an imagination I had. Her sister worked as a waitress and would bring home the pads she used to write orders down on, and we got to use them to play with. That was really cool and exciting to us. We would use all the dishes to play restaurant with. Our parents were so patient with us. Our childhood and pretending was simply magical. I had never been so happy.

We loved to play board games such as Monopoly, Big Deal, Sorry, Battleship, Candyland, Chutes and Ladders, Yahtzee, Bingo, Checkers, Parcheesi, Chinese Checkers, Clue, Dominoes, Scrabble, and the Addams Family. This game was set up that whoever finished first would lose the game and they would die and have a tombstone. We would always hate to die. We would try and keep the game going and going and going. No one wanted to lose or die.

We played jacks, pick up sticks, and different card games. Some of them were Uno, Skip-Bo Uno, Bid Euchre, War, Slap Jack, Old Maid, and Go Fish. We loved to jump rope and sing songs too. One time we didn't have enough people so we tied the one end of the jump rope to the door handle and one of us would swing the rope while the other jumped and then we would switch places. We also played with hula hoops.

We rarely ever fought, and if we did it was very minor, and we always said we were sorry and forgave each other right away. We would write notes to each other saying, "I sorry."

We loved watching the *Wizard of Oz* when it came on the television once a year in the spring. Time seemed to stand still and life was just great.

I really liked my second grade teacher. We are still in contact today. I had self-doubts about my answers on tests. The teacher told my parents at the parent-teacher conference that I would write the right answer down on the test and then would erase it and change it. She said I needed to stick with my first answer. I remember sitting in class one time and felt something on the back of my neck. I pulled it off, and it was a wood tick. I remember screaming right in the middle of class, "Wood tick, wood tick, wood tick!" The teacher stopped what she was doing, came to my desk, and helped me to get rid of it.

Through all of this, I was slowly growing up.

Chapter 7

GETTING OLDER

We started joining groups outside of school. We were in 4H, Girl Scouts, and Jet Cadets on Wednesday at a local church. I sewed my own skirt in 4H and got a blue ribbon for it at the fair. I remember at Bible school we would play Red Rover and Hopscotch. When third grade came, I liked the teacher but I struggled in her class. It was a tough year for me but a fun one all at the same time. Our teacher introduced us to an album called *Free to Be You and Me*. I loved it, and years later, I found it and have it today. I am still in contact with this teacher as well today.

The holidays were magical. At Halloween, we would all dress up in our costumes, get in line, and march through the cafeteria for everyone to see us or through all the different classrooms. We would then have a party back in our classrooms. We had cookies and juice and would dunk for apples. My neighbor would always give me a popcorn ball for trick or treat. I would take a pillowcase and go from town to town, getting as much candy as I could before the time was up. It would be after dark and last several hours. Then my parents would have to check all of our candy for razor blades and pins before we could eat it.

At Thanksgiving, we would have a play and dress up like pilgrims. At Christmas, we decorated a plate for a Christmas present for our moms. Mine was a Christmas tree. It was dated as well. One time we took apples and put cloves all over it to preserve it and make an air freshener.

In January we made snowflakes, and in February we talked about George Washington and Abraham Lincoln's birthdays. We also made our own Valentine envelopes and exchanged Valentine cards with everyone in the classroom. We also got candy, cookies, and juice.

There was this blond-headed boy in our class that all the girls thought was cute. I had such a crush on him. At recess, we would play on the hill, and once he kissed me on the lips. I couldn't believe that it really happened, and I was never so excited in my whole life. In our class pictures, he was beside me and I thought that was great. I knew where he lived because he rode my bus, but I never went there.

In art, we made hook rugs. The boy sat by me and talked to me when he wasn't supposed to, so we both got in trouble and had to get two whacks with the wooden paddle with the holes in it. We had to bend over and hold our ankles. The art teacher did it after our art class, and going back to class was so humiliating. I wanted to just hide in the coatroom. Because of this, the boy and I talked about becoming superheroes and busting out of school. That was the first and only time that happened.

I struggled with math in this grade. I never really learned how to add and subtract and am still not the best at it today. In fourth grade, I had the same teacher that my brothers had. She was old but she was good. She had a habit of spitting on you when she talked. Not one of her students left her classroom until we all knew how to multiply and divide. Today, I still do this better than adding and subtracting. This teacher retired the next year.

In fifth grade, our teacher would have us pray in the classroom after we lined up for lunch. We would go to the cafeteria for lunch, and the teacher who dismissed each table would say, "Act like a tree and leave." Our teacher always wore heals, and to not make a noise when walking, she would always walk on her toes. She had a big white smile. She was another teacher I really liked. She quoted a poem in my autograph book once that said, "Good, better, best. Never let it rest. Until your good is better, and your better, best."

This was also the year I broke both of my arms on different occasions. I will explain more about that later. Music class was always fun. I remember the flutophones/recorders. I will never forget those plastic noisemakers. That was fun stuff. I loved singing in music class. I remember it seemed like we screamed "We Three Kings of

Orient Are" at Christmas. I would sit next to the boy I had a crush on in third grade and got in trouble with. We would scream it together.

In sixth grade, I had my first male teacher. I remember he was missing his fingers on his one hand and his elbows were always dry, brown, and crusty. He kept a Nerf ball in his desk, and while we were doing homework, he would sneak it out and throw it at one of us. We would throw it back, and he would throw it at another student. He would throw an eraser at us if we weren't behaving. He came across as very stern, but was really a lot of fun.

Oh, and gym class was fun too. I loved dodge ball, kick ball, the parachute, the trampoline, the scooter on wheels, doing some gymnastics, square dancing, and climbing ropes among a few.

Once a year, near the end of the school year, when it was nice out, we would have field day. It was all day, and we would go outside to have it. We would sign up for the events you wanted to do. I did the one-hundred-yard dash, the sack race, the obstacle course, and the egg toss. It was so fun. I was in good shape and did very well in the events. They handed out ribbons, and I got quite a few blue ribbons, which was first place. I also got on the honor roll a lot in school. I was not necessarily a straight-A student though.

At recess, we had a really cool merry-go-round that would go really fast, teeter-totters, slides, swings, and monkey bars. We would love to go outside and play on them. I learned to hang upside down on the monkey bars and cross them skipping a bar at a time. I learned you had to get your swing on. When we were upside down on them, we would grab arms with someone on the ground, lift them, and swing them.

We had a hill to slide down on in the winter too. It was the hill from my first kiss as well as my broken arm (more on the broken arm to follow). The school also had fallout shelters, and at recess we would go and explore them.

As time went on, I was getting older.

Chapter 8

NOTHING LIKE FRIENDS

Up until sixth grade, my best friend and I since second grade were inseparable. She was the sister I never had. I did have a neighbor boy across the street, and we would hang out and ride bikes together. My best friend and I would go to the fireworks together and the fair. The fireworks were being shot off so close that when we laid there it looked like they were going to land on us and we would giggle. We did a lot of laughing together, sometimes even when we weren't supposed to, like church and in the bathroom of a restaurant when someone was in there and we didn't know it at first. This would make us laugh even more.

One year, as we got older, we worked in the lemonade stand together at the fair. That is when I learned how to count change back. It was so much fun except for the bees. They loved the sugar. My arms hurt too, from all the shaking. My best friend and I were part of each other's families by now. She would go to church with me and my family and I did the same with hers. I was invited over for her sibling's birthday parties. She had one sister and four brothers. Her mom always made the best birthday cakes. I loved her meatloaf and Spanish rice, also.

I will never forget when they had me for Christmas. It was fun watching everyone open their gifts. This was all new to me because we didn't do that at our house. Her mom got me a stocking with stocking stuffers in it. I had never received anything like that, so I was so excited. I got a book of candy Life Savers and I loved it.

They lived in an old big two-story brick farm home. They had a barn with a horse and pigs. They had two dogs and a cat. They had a big rock in the front yard we would climb on. Their one dog and cat would have puppies and kittens.

Her mom smoked at the time, and she loved Pepsi. Once in a while, she would let us have some of her Pepsi, and it was a great treat. One time, we took cigarette buds from the ashtray and took them upstairs to my friend's bedroom, lit them, and tried to smoke them. I didn't really like them. Smoking never became one of my things.

We were scared of graveyards and the picture her mom had. It was a painting of her mom from when she was younger, and my friend and I both thought it resembled Mona Lisa. We thought the eyes moved. My friend thought she saw a funny man in the window once too.

Sixth grade brought about a lot of changes. My oldest brother, the truck driver, had been divorced and would come home from time to time with his semi. He dated a very pretty lady with a son. We got to meet them, and I thought the son was good looking. We only met them the one time, and my brother didn't date her anymore for whatever reason. He then came home with a woman who had really long dark hair and two daughters. This relationship was more serious, and they got married and lived with us.

I was in hopes of a better relationship with my brother, but the semi still took him away. I now had to share my bedroom and my time with the daughters. The one daughter was my age and in the same grade. As I worked on trying to make them feel welcomed, my friendship with my best friend suffered. Eventually, my brother moved a house trailer in behind our house, and I got my bedroom back. It was a time of adjustment for us all.

The family living in my grandpa's house had a daughter one year younger than me, and the girl across the street was one year older. We would all get together and swim or run around the yards. My best friend would come over too. This was when tag, freeze tag, and hide-and-seek became really fun. Our quiet, lonely neighborhood changed to having not just one friend, but a whole group of kids.

One time, we were all swimming in our pond when the neighbor girl panicked in the deep end and grabbed my best friend. They were both going under. I swam to the edge, climbed out, and ran to get the life preserver. I threw it in to reach the girl panicking. As she let go of my best friend, my best friend swam to the edge as well as the girl. No one drowned, thank goodness. It was very scary.

We had bought an outside tent, and all of us would stay in there by the pond at night. My best friend and I loved to play spy. We would spy on my family. We even set up my tape recorder so my family didn't know and recorded them talking. We could hear it when we played it back, my mom telling my brother to "pull up his breeches" and we would laugh. One time when we were in the tent, the neighbor boy, a mile over, came over on a moped and was walking around the tent with a helmet on. I thought he was an alien from outer space. One time I thought I really saw a flying saucer above our yard.

I liked to play cowboys and Indians, and loved to play with racetracks, farm animals, and army men. I had a red wagon, and it had rained and water was in it. I bent over and got my hair wet, pretending I was washing it. My mom got my picture doing it. I loved drinking water from the garden hose as well. We had a three-wheeled bike with a basket on it. We loved to ride that around. It seemed like it took me forever to learn how to ride a bike, but one day it took ahold and I was riding.

The same thing happened with swimming. I was scared of the water at first. I went with the neighbors across the street before they moved. We went to a lake. They had me walk out to the deep where you couldn't touch, and I went under, panicked, and went back to the shallow. With a life jacket, I practiced in the pond. One day, I took it off and I was swimming by myself.

The people that lived in my grandpa's house were also foster parents. They took in a boy for a while. We became good friends, and when I learned he was leaving, it was hard. He gave me a kiss, and it was not just on the lips. It was my first French kiss. It was a kiss good-bye. I went home crying.

There was certainly nothing like friends.

Chapter 9

ENTERTAINMENT

As I was now older, I made more and more friends. I would stay the night with them or they would stay the night with me. My dad had a riding lawn mower, and my friends and I would drive it all around the yard. It was fun. One time we ran into a tree, but the lawn mower and my friend and I were okay.

In the winter, when there was snow, we would make trails and dig out a spot to call our den. We would play fox and rabbit. It was basically tag but you had to stay on the trails. You were safe if you made it back to your den. If the fox caught you or you fell out of the trails, then you became the fox. I would knock down icicles from the roof of the house and chew on them. I would pretend when I was the rabbit that the icicle was my carrot. I also ate snow and caught snowflakes on my tongue. I had such an imagination.

The neighbor next door had a big hill behind the barn that went to the creek. We would take our sleds and ride down the hill for hours. They had an electric fence, though. Once I hit it when it was on, and it was awful with the jolt going through my body. I can remember still sledding even when it was getting dark. It was cold, quiet, and crisp, and the moon shined down on the white snow, making everything glow while the snow fell all around us.

One year, I got to have a birthday party and I was able to invite guys and girls. We were outside playing kissing tag. If a guy caught a girl, they had to kiss each other. One guy tried to grab me where I didn't want to be grabbed, and so that ended the game abruptly. We all went back into the house after that. I did have an all-girl birthday party one time when I was younger.

Since we had the pond, in the winter, my dad would drill a hole in the ice for the fish to breathe, and to see how thick the ice was. That is where I learned to ice skate. I wasn't ready for the Olympics, but I could hold my own. I could cross my legs around the curves going forward and backward as well. I always wanted to throw an ice skating party where I would decorate all the pine trees in white lights, play music, ice skate, and have hot cocoa. I never got to do that.

I could also do this with roller skates. I had the roller skates down better than the ice skates, though. My friends and I would go on the weekends to the roller rink. They had where you could go Friday night and stay until Sunday evening. It was all day and all night, and we would stay awake and skate, skate, and skate some more. They played music, and we could skate with the lights on, or they would have it dark with disco lights. They made it dark with slow songs, and it was couples only on the floor. It was a marble floor. It hurt when you fell. They also had spin the bottle and limbo. It was always a good time.

The music era was seventies and eighties. I also listened to country music. Solid Gold and American Bandstand with Dick Clark were on TV at the time. I would listen to Casey Kasem's Top Countdown list on the radio. I would even tape it with cassette tapes.

I lived for Saturdays and the Saturday morning cartoons. That was the best thing ever. Some of the shows I would watch were *The Smurfs*, *Scooby-Doo*, *Looney Tunes*, *The Flintstones*, *The Jetsons*, *Fat Albert*, and *Land of the Lost*. It was wonderful.

During the week on TV, early in the morning was *Captain Kangaroo*. He had Mr. Green Jeans, Bunny Rabbit, Mr. Moose, and the Grandfather Clock. I loved that show. *Patches & Pockets* were also on early in the morning. They were two clowns. Sundays, *Davey and Goliath* were on. Davey was a boy and Goliath was his dog. It was a good show. The once-a-year shows at Christmas I loved were *Rudolph the Red-Nosed Reindeer* and *Frosty the Snowman*. In the spring, I loved *Here Comes Peter Cottontail*.

Our TV was a floor console and had a remote control. This was a new concept. The first time we had ever seen or used a remote control. The TV was in color too. The channels would change by responding to a certain noise the controller would make. If you passed your channel, you had to go through all the channels again to get to the one you wanted. I remember one time when we were eating and the silverware were clicking together, the TV channels changed on their own. It freaked us out until we figured it out. Then we would take the silverware to the living room and bang them together to get the TV to change channels. It didn't take much to entertain us. Once, I thought I saw something coming at me from out of the TV. Once again, it was just my creative imagination.

I also remember watching Sonny and Cher. I loved Cher. I thought she was cool with that long dark hair. My mother had a different opinion. Other favorite shows and movies of mine were *Wild Kingdom*, Walt Disney films, *Laverne & Shirley*, *Three's Company, Happy Days with the Fonz (eyy)*, *Sha Na Na*, *Welcome Back*, *The Brady Bunch*, *Bewitched*, *I Dream of Jeannie*, *I Love Lucy*, *Family Affair, Hawaii Five-O*, *Love Boat*, *Fantasy Island*, *Gilligan's Island*, *Rockford Files*, *Kojak*, *The Tonight Show with Johnny Carson*, *The Phil Donahue Show*, *The Six Million Dollar Man*, *The Incredible Hulk*, *Batman, Godzilla*, *King Kong*, *Ghostbusters*, *ET*, *The Gong Show*, *Family Feud, The $100,000 Pyramid*, *Hollywood Squares*, *The Dating Game*, *Name That Tune*, *Little House on the Prairie*, *The Walton's*, *The Partridge Family*, *Donny and Marie Osmond*, *Eight is Enough*, *The Price is Right*, *Dukes of Hazard*, *BJ and The Bear*, *Gremlins*, *Lassie*, *Benji*, *The Shaggy Dog*, *Herby*, *The Apple Dumpling Gang*, *Porky's*, *Fast Times at Ridgemont High*, *Top Gun*, *Risky Business*, *Officer and a Gentleman, Mannequin*, *The Breakfast Club*, *Splash*, and *Ferris Buehler's Day Off*.

In *What's Happening*, there was J.J. Walker who always said the hit line Dynamite. In *Different Strokes*, there was Arnold, that cute, chubby-cheeked boy, who always said the hit line, "Whatcha talking about Willis?" In *Sanford and Son*, the old man would always fake a heart attack and say, "I'm coming to see you, Elizabeth," as he held his hand on his chest and stumbled around like he was going to fall over. More shows and actors included, The *Jeffersons*, *All in the Family*, *Alice*, *Flo* (kiss my grits), *Facts of Life*, *One Day at a Time*, Mary Tyler Moore, Carol Burnett, Barbra Mandrel, Dolly Parton, *The Little Rascals*, *Leave it to Beaver*, *The Andy Griffith Show*, *Gomer*

Pyle, U.S.M.C. (ga-ah-ly), *The Smothers Brothers Comedy Hour,* and M*A*S*H.

Later on came, *Full House, Family Ties, Step by Step, The Cosby Show, Golden Girls, Designing Women, Murphy Brown, Seventh Heaven, Friends, Seinfeld, Cheers, Touched By An Angel, Murder She Wrote, Bob Newhart Show* (This is my brother Larry, Darrel, and my other brother Darrel), *WKRP in Cincinnati, Everybody Loves Raymond, The Nanny, Home Improvement, Dallas* (Who shot JR?), *Dynasty, Twin Peaks, ER, Chicago Hope, Adam 12, Chips,* Magic shows, Evel Knievel, Circus, The Harlem Globetrotters, *Mister Rogers's Neighborhood, Sesame Street, School House Rock, Zoom, The Mickey Mouse Club, Xenia, Planet of the Apes, Zorro,* and *The Bionic Woman* with Lindsey Wagner. She was my idol. Superwoman was Linda Carter. As I got older, *Guiding Light* was my favorite soap opera, and I would watch *Oprah.* TV was a big influence in my life. My first movie at a movie theater was *Charlotte's Web.* I went with a friend from school.

That was entertainment at its best.

Chapter 10

CHRISTMAS AT HOME, MY STUFF, AND MY BEDROOM

At Christmas, we had a tree, stockings, wreath, and big lights that were colored for the bush in front of the big window outside the front of our house. We didn't get presents at Christmas. Dad would give us a card with a two-dollar bill inside. That would be all we would get. Our stockings were just decorations, and nothing was ever put in them as gifts.

I never received presents for my birthday either. Dad would buy things for me from time to time at the store if I wanted something. I didn't get a lot, but the things I did get meant a lot to me.

I remember I had a baby doll but I lost it. I was so upset and begged my dad to go to the store to get me another one. After begging enough, my dad gave in, only to get home to find the other doll. Oops! I ended up with twin baby dolls.

I loved my Easy Bake Oven. I remember tossing the dough before cooking it. It ended up on the ceiling of the utility room where I was playing with it and got stuck. It finally fell off. I think it left a stain on the ceiling though.

I also loved my little red wooden rocking chair that I still have. I had a couple Barbie Dolls with some outfits and a Barbie case. I also had some blow-up furniture for them. When I got older, I got a record player and records, a radio with a cassette tape player/recorder, a phone in my room, a bulletin board with tacks, a TV, and my first car. We also had a tent, and I had a sleeping bag and stuffed animals.

I remember my great aunt let me borrow her pink wicker baby buggy to play with. I would dress the cats up in my doll clothes, wrap them in blankets, and put them in the buggy. I would push them down the sidewalk. They didn't like that at all.

I remember when we brought my swing set home. It was put on the roof of our car. My father was helping to tie it down. He walked right into the bottom of the metal pole, hitting his glasses straight on, and the glass shattered and went into his eye. He was not happy about that at all. He did get all the glass out of his eye.

When I got into high school, my father bought me a desk, chair, and typewriter as well. My first bedroom was the closest one to the living room. My bed was a twin and had a brown wooden headboard, and I had Flintstone curtains. Pebbles and Bam Bam were on them. Later, my brother and I switched bedrooms. My room was now closer to my mother and father's room at the end of the hall. It was in the back corner of the house, and I had two windows. One of the windows was on the side of the house and one on the back of the house. My brother kept my twin bed, and I ended up getting a double bed with a brass headboard. The curtains ended up in the laundry room.

My room had pink plaster walls and burgundy carpet. The ceiling was white plaster, and I had a ceiling light. The curtains were floor length with a ruffle and tie backs. They were pink with burgundy flowers on them. I had a nightstand with my lamp that my brother made and my alarm clock. It was the kind that each number would flip over and it lit up. I had a floor-length mirror on the wall by my closet door. I had a dresser and a metal cabinet in the corner to put my games in. I put my TV on the top of it so I could watch TV in my bed without any problems. I had a remote control for it. It was just a small TV. I had the phone hung on the wall in my room. We had a phone in the living room and one on our back glassed-in porch as well.

A few other things that occupied my time that I had were a ball-in-hole game, a picture mix up, a ring catch, a yo-yo, a slinky, and Play-Doh. I liked blowing bubbles too. I had an electronic game called Blip. It was like playing ping-pong. I also read books and did the find a wordbooks. My brother and I would also play hide the thimble. We would say if we were hot or cold. If we were getting close to finding the thimble, we would say you're getting hot and the further away, we would say you are getting cold.

All in all, I enjoyed the things I had.

Chapter 11

GROWING PAINS

The first time I remember being in the hospital overnight for a few days was when I was in early elementary school for an illness. It was Easter time in 1974, and I was six years old. I was still young enough that I hadn't spent the night away from my parents. I remember being scared to death when they left me to go home and didn't stay with me. They put me in this really big crib, which I hated, because I was in a regular bed at home. They even put a net on top to keep me in. I hated, hated, hated that! I missed my mom and dad and just wanted to go home.

I remember the time seemed to stand still as the days went by, and my parents would stop in to see me only to leave without me again. When they came, it didn't seem like they stayed very long. I remember finally, one day, the nurse said that I would get to go home that day. I was so excited and couldn't wait for my parents to come and get me. I waited and waited, but they didn't show up. Another nurse came on duty and I asked if I was going home and she said no. I remember crying and crying and crying in that stupid crib they had me in. I wanted to go home and go home now. While I had my back to the door all curled up in a fetal position, crying, I turned around to my surprise and there were my parents. To make things even better, they were there to take me home. Little did I know that this experience was to prepare me for my future.

On the way home, we stopped at a local restaurant. I had a bowl of vegetable soup. Later when we were home, people from our church came by and brought me this huge Easter coloring book the size of me for a get-well gift. I remember absolutely loving that book.

I took it to my bedroom, put it on my bed, and started coloring in it, chewing bubble gum at the same time and trying to learn how to blow bubbles. I was eventually able to blow a bubble inside a bubble without popping them. How fun! I still have that coloring book in my closet today. It meant the world to me, and funny thing is, it still does today. Something I will never forget.

So now this leads me to my first set of stitches. I had my best friend over, and my mom and dad said we were going to my brother's to see my nieces and nephews who were my age and that my best friend could come along. I was so excited because this would be the first time they would meet each other. Well, I became a little too excited. I started running through the house, out the side screen door leading to the garage, and reaching for the outside door handle to only miss and rammed my right arm all the way through the glass window, breaking it. There was a huge sharp pointed edge of glass on the top that when I went to pull my arm back through, I sliced my arm wide open at two locations. One was worse than the other. It had sliced so deep that you could see all the layers of skin and muscle, and it must have hit an artery or something because every time my heart would beat, it would shoot blood straight out. I was bleeding like mad, and dad wrapped a towel around my arm to soak up the blood. Somehow, I just knew this was more than a Band-Aid moment, and now our trip to my nieces and nephews would be a trip to the emergency room instead. What a big disappointment after so much excitement. So off to the hospital we went.

When we got to the closest hospital, another lady was waiting in the waiting room to get in. She felt I was much worse and let me go in front of her. I think my best friend's mom came and picked my best friend up from the hospital. When I got in, they took a needle and thread and they sewed my arm up. I think four stitches in one spot and five in the deep one. My arm did heal fine, leaving a couple of scars permanently for a constant reminder of that day. Little did I know this was only a little touch of how pain can feel. While still in the hospital, I remember they had a gumball machine, but the gum was square like Chiclets and they were white mint ones. Dad would give me change out of his pocket so I could get some. I also remember the bathroom at the hospital. The door was wooden, very heavy, and narrow. It was on an air spring. The floors were a marble tile, cold and hard.

On another occasion, my family liked to go to another restaurant in the town a half hour away. When I was little, I loved mashed potatoes a lot, so my parents would order them for me. I still love them today. The waitress asked my mother and father if I was their granddaughter, and they would smile and tell her I was their daughter. The restaurant had these really big heavy metal doors. The handles were long rod iron spirals. When we were leaving, I got a toothpick. I put it in my mouth. My father was in front of me. He opened up the big door to go out and he didn't realize I was right behind him, and the door slammed shut on my face, shoving the toothpick down my throat. I remember it hurt so bad and was so sharp and poky in my throat. I don't recall how we got it out or if I swallowed it. I just remember it hurt really bad. That building is still there with the same doors. It is a Chinese restaurant now.

Now what is a hospital stay for an illness, stitches, and a toothpick down the throat without some broken bones to add to the list. I swear I got hurt more often than my three brothers put together. I don't know if that qualifies me as a real tomboy or just a big klutz. The worst my brothers had besides the tractor accident was jumping over barbwire fences, ripping their clothes or skin or trying to catch a nest of baby skunks and got sprayed.

Well, for the story of my broken bones. Here goes. I was at my brother's house playing with my nieces and nephews. It was the summer before fifth grade, and we were playing in the backyard on the swing set. Things were going great until my niece hurt her toe. My sister-in-law gets her in the car, and they go off to the hospital. Now my brother was there watching us, and we resumed playing on the swings. I was pretending to be the *Bionic Woman*. Lindsey Wagner was my idol. I still think she is so pretty today. So there I was, swinging and swinging and swinging, trying to get as high as possible. So now I was up there pretty good and I decided to jump out of the swing when I get my highest so I can be just like the *Bionic Woman*.

Well, the landing didn't work out so well for me. When you are a kid, you just don't understand the power of gravity. I'll learn that lesson more than once as a kid. More on that a little bit later. When I landed, I landed with my left arm pinned between the ground and my knee. At first, I got up and thought I was okay and then I felt this huge stinging in my arm. I looked down and tried to move it but I couldn't. When I looked down, the area between the wrist and the elbow was completely deformed. The skin was just hanging like a big dip on a rollercoaster ride. I started screaming, "I broke my arm, I broke my arm."

We went running in the house to get my brother. He had me sit down and started making phone calls. If I remember correctly, we waited for my sister-in-law to get home with my niece. She had broken her toe. My sister-in-law took me to the nearest hospital. I remember the X-ray technician wanting me to flip my arm over to get an X-ray, and I just couldn't do it no matter how hard I tried. I was in so much pain. They ended up sending me to another hospital. When I got there, they explained to me that I completely snapped both main bones in my arm clear through. Ouch! Now for my first time of experiencing utter and complete pain.

They had to set my arm. Oh my gosh! I had no idea how bad this was going to hurt. The nurse stood on my right and held my right hand, telling me to squeeze her hand as tight as I want. They took my left arm. They raised it up so my hand was pointing toward the sky and they pulled straight up, trying to get both bones back on top of each other. They did not tell me any of this, and I had no idea what they were doing. It hurt so darn bad. They then laid my arm back down on my stomach. They came back with a bucket and gloves. Still being left in the dark, in pain, and scared to death, I whimpered, "What are you going to do to me *now*?"

They said, "Oh it is okay, honey. The worst is all over. We are going to put your cast on now." I thought they couldn't do anything with my arm so they brought the bucket and gloves and were going to get a saw and cut my arm off and throw it in the bucket. Wow, was I glad I asked and glad that wasn't the case at all. What a relief! Okay, now I could breathe a little.

Wow, what things we think of as a kid, a great imagination. Pain can make you think all kinds of stuff. Okay, so now for my cast. They mixed up the white Plaster of Paris and soaked the wrap in it and started wrapping it around my arm. They went up to just under my armpit all the way down, wrapping around my wrist and hand, only leaving my fingers and thumb out.

I couldn't go swimming the rest of the summer. I couldn't let it get wet. I remember how hot and sweaty it got and how my skin itched. I would find all kinds of objects to try and stick in my cast to get to the itch—a pen, ruler, coat hanger. I had to wear that thing for six months, until both bones had healed all the way back together again.

When it was time to take the cast off, they only took part of it at a time. They cut the top part off first with a saw. Here was when the saw part comes in. I was still scared they would get too close to my skin, and a couple times they did, nicking my skin, but they didn't cut my arm off and throw it in a bucket. They cut the part off from under my armpit to just below the elbow so I could do exercises to get my elbow to bend and straighten again. My skin was all old and peeling and falling off, leaving my skin all pink. It was gross. Soon after, the rest of my cast was taken off and I practiced moving my wrist again.

Everything was just getting back to normal when *bang!* Within the same calendar year, only the seasons changed from summer to winter, I go and break my other arm. This time it was my right arm. I was in fifth grade now, and we were out for recess. I had my brand-new snowmobile suit on, and we were sliding down the hill by the sewers. Same place I got my kiss in third grade. I started running, and when I hit the hill—which was covered in ice, hard as a rock—I had this bad feeling I was going to break my arm. Sure enough, I came down on my right arm. When I got up, I could tell I broke it because it felt just like the way my other arm felt when I broke it.

Now my best friend helped walk me to the office holding my arm. They could not get my snowmobile suit off. They put a blow up brace over my arm, and I waited for someone to come and get me. They tried to call my parents, but they were gone, with my father at work selling his oil. That was way before cell phones. They got ahold of my aunt. She came with a pillow. My uncle was teasing me like he always did. He asked me if I slipped on a banana peel. I rode in the backseat with my arm on the pillow while they took me to the doctor. This doctor sent me right onto a big hospital in a city in another state over.

My parents finally arrived at the hospital with my oldest brother, which surprised me. I guess he was home off the semi. My mother was so worried that I broke the same arm all over again. They ended up cutting my snowmobile suit off me. Brand-new and the first time I ever wore it. I was not too happy about that. They ran X-rays, and sure enough, just like the other arm, both main bones were completely snapped into two. The good thing this time was they put me out to set my arm so I wouldn't feel the pain. Here I go with the whole cast thing again now for another six months. I had to go back and forth to this city to keep seeing the doctor.

Going back to school now was not easy since I was right-handed. I had to use my left hand, and the teacher also gave me an assistant to help write my answers down for me. I was also learning to play the trumpet in music. I got so far behind, so I dropped out from playing it any more. My arm does finally heal, and I was doing better until I go to my nieces and nephews to play again.

This time they lived in the country with a barn. We all were playing tag in the hay mound. There was some loose straw on the floor, and I hit it just right and slid as if I was on ice and went over the edge headfirst. I dropped to the level below me. The only time I had this sensation was diving into water, so I automatically plugged my nose. I very quickly came to my senses and realized I'm not hitting water but cement. When I hit, I hit so hard on my neck and spine. It knocked the air out of me, and I could not breathe.

This only happened one other time when I was younger, falling down the neighbors steps. It is so scary when you feel like you can't breathe. I hated that feeling. I had just missed the tractor. The other kids were laughing at me because I plugged my nose. I tried really hard to get myself together and shake it all off and kept on moving as to not let anyone know how much pain I was in. I came around finally and we never told an adult. Boy I was really stupid and should have been checked out at the hospital but I didn't.

Later on during school, they checked kids for scoliosis, a curve of the spine, and sure enough I had it. I know it was from that fall. My body was just taking a beating like never before.

I also had a lot of stomachaches. My father gave me peppermint extract, and it worked. I would get sore throats, and my father would rub Vicks on my chest and wrap a handkerchief around my neck. I would get a lot of ear infections too until I discovered that if I got water in them, the water wouldn't drain and it caused the infections. From then on, I would always wear earplugs in the shower or when I swam, and it fixed the problem.

When I was around five years old, I fell down the steps at the neighbor's house across the street. I was at the very top stair and fell down the whole way and hit my spine. The fall knocked the air out of me, and I could not breathe. It was a very scary feeling, but it finally subsided. I never went to the doctor to check it out. After the second time of hitting my spine, falling out of the hay mound, I realized that will knock the air out of you when you hit your spine like that.

One time at a boy/girl party when I was a little older, I was chased by a swarm of bees. It was in the country by a woods, and I somehow entered into their presence. They would not stop chasing me, and I could not get away from them. I ran and ran and ran. But the more I ran, the more they chased me. I was terrified! Finally, they just stopped, and I was unharmed.

Needless to say, I took my growing pains to the extreme.

Chapter 12

PETS:
WANTED AND UNWANTED

My first dog was given to me by my youngest brother. He brought him home to me. I named him Sockie. He was white with big brown circles on him. He was a short-haired small dog. He had ears that flopped over. We had a doghouse for him. We think he died because our neighbor shot him. I was so upset about that.

My cat was calico. I named her Calie. We also had a lot of outdoor cats. My mom would feed them milk and cat food. She would call them, "Here, Kitty, Kitty, Kitty. Kitty, Kitty, Kitty. Kitty, Kitty, Kitty. Kitty, Kitty, Kitty." They would all come running from all the neighbors. It was neat how my mom had them all trained to come when she called them.

After Sockie died, my parents got me a grey schnauzer. I named her Candy. She got to stay inside the house with us. We got her from the pound. She was a wonderful dog. She was my dog for the rest of my childhood.

One day, one of our cats was at the end of our driveway, hiding in the Fostoria bush right by the road, when a motorcycle was approaching. The engine sound scared the cat. It jumped straight up out of the bush and right into the guy's windshield, breaking the cat's neck, instantly killing it. We had to bury it. The guy stopped. It scared the crap out of him and then he felt really bad. Glad the guy was okay, though.

At another time, we had a cat that would love to climb up in the engine of our car to keep warm. My father went to start the car up, and the cat came flying out from underneath the hood. It had got its tail and ear caught in the fan belt and it lost part of its tail and ear. But it lived through it all. My father felt so bad, and we had to check under the hood for cats from then on before starting the car.

I was so afraid that our cats would get hit on the road, so I tried to keep them locked up in the shed, but it only made the shed stink really bad. It was not a healthy environment for them anyways. A lesson I had to learn. Sometimes you just have to let go. Something once again preparing me for my future.

In the summer, I would love to chase lightning bugs and put them in a jar like all little kids do. We also had these tree frogs that would stick to our front screen door window with their suction cup feet. It was when we had the glass part of the window in and not the screen part.

Our front step had a crack in it. One time, a garter snake was lying in it. I screamed. I do not like snakes. I would jump over that step from then on. We had really big spiders also, and I did not like them either. So this leads me into pets that were not wanted. I am so scarred for life with the next two stories I'm about to tell you. Do you know, which I believe is true, that mice multiply faster than rabbits?

One day, my father saw a mouse running through the kitchen. He decided to follow it to see where it was going to set a trap for it. While searching for the mouse that ran into the kitchen cupboards, my father opened a drawer that was not used very often, only to find a whole nest of full-grown mice! He made my brother help him carry the drawer of mice outside to the fire pit to get rid of the mice. When my father opened another drawer, it was filled with half-grown mice! So by now my father was opening everything up and discovering another drawer full of newborn little tiny pink baby mice with no hair! I wanted to be in the kitchen to see what was going on but then again I didn't. I didn't want to touch the floor and have a mouse run over my feet. So there I was, sitting on top of the kitchen table, watching all the action.

As my father and brother took these mice outside, my mother took everything out of all the cupboards and washes everything down. My father actually set the mice on fire in the fire pit. They were running up the walls of the fire pit, squealing and trying to get out. I felt so bad because I didn't want them to die or at least die like that, but I didn't want them in the house or coming back into the house. After all this work, we realized we still haven't got the mouse that started this search in the first place yet.

I was still sitting on the kitchen table when they were getting ready to put the last drawer back in. I was getting ready to tell them to put it back in so the mouse couldn't get out and it would go to the trap, when the mouse came jumping out and almost landed on the kitchen table with me. I went running and screaming to the top of my lungs into the other part of the house. We did catch him in the trap later.

I could not sleep after that knowing we were sharing our home with all of those mice and wondering did we really get them all. That was simply bad, bad, bad, bad, and bad. Nothing like having the creepy crawlies and wondering if they ran over you at night while you slept. Not good. Not good at all. Bad, bad, bad. It still gives me the creeps just thinking about it. Those newborn mice were really, really ugly too. Everything, and I mean everything about that whole situation was very disturbing. Now if that isn't bad enough, my next story really isn't much better.

Another time, I came home later in the evening and everyone was asleep. I went into the bathroom to go potty. We had shower doors that slid shut on the tub. You could not see through them. They were closed at the time. I was sitting there when I heard this splashing noise. I asked if someone was there, and there was no answer. I still kept hearing the splashing noise, so I slowly slide the door and tried to peek in, only to find the whole tub full of catfish. I started screaming to the top of my lungs, thinking the whole time, "What the heck was that all about? Fish in the bathtub! Am I going crazy or what? That is just not right!" I started screaming for dad. He came running in. I was so scared all I could do was point.

He put too much copper sulfate in the pond, and so the fish started floating because they were not getting enough oxygen. These catfish were my dad's babies, so my dad and brother scoop up all the fish and bring them into the house and put them in the bathtub to keep them alive. They survived it and were put back in the pond. I, however, will probably never be the same again.

These were our pets, whether we wanted them or not.

Chapter 13

JUNIOR HIGH AND HIGH SCHOOL

This is now the time in my life for a lot of changes. There were changes in classrooms at school, changes in teachers, changes in friends, changes of my body, and changes in my family, changes, changes, and more changes.

In junior high, we would go to a different classroom with a different teacher for every subject. We had two different buildings in two different towns. Both buildings had your lower grade levels. The building I was in held the junior high for both locations, so a bunch of new kids came to join us. The high school was at the other building in the next town over. Our music class now turned into choir, and we had dances. My best friend from second grade moved, and I became close to another girl. I always stayed the night at her house; though, she never came to mine.

I loved going to the fair. One time I got off a ride and noticed blood on the inside of my leg. I went to the bathroom to look closer. I thought I cut my leg on the ride. Little did I know, because it was not really talked about much then, I was becoming a woman. Who would have thought? Welcome to womanhood.

I also discovered my first love. He was a grade above me. We first started out mainly as phone buddies. We could talk for hours about everything and anything. This went on for months. My first love and I started to become closer and get creative, finding any way we could to see each other outside of school. These hookups turned into secret make-out sessions.

We met up at the fairgrounds and would go inside the tractors or combines displayed at the fair. We would meet at the park and go in the tunnels. We went to the dugouts at the school and in the school buses that were parked. We went behind the auditorium and down into the industrial arts room in the high school. We went behind the post office and the mill. Everywhere we could find, we made out.

I loved the way he smelled. I will always remember that scent and how great it felt to be in his arms. We had so much fun, and I loved him so much. We were in track together and choir. He played the piano and the trombone.

Then during my freshman year of high school, he came over with his moped, picked me up, and took me back to his place. His parents were gone, so we took advantage of that and made out in his bedroom with the radio on.

The song playing was "We've Got Tonight." It is amazing how a song can all of a sudden become a song with so much meaning in your life at a specific time or event with only certain people and that song becomes a treasure locked away in your memory and heart and can only apply to that given time, place, and person.

I started to want more from the relationship. I wanted to shout it out to the world and let everyone know we were a couple. Even though the sneaking around was fun, I started to feel we had just become a dirty little secret; I did not want that any longer, so I broke our relationship off.

He started hanging around a couple girls just as friends, but I felt he flaunted his friendships with them in front of me to make me jealous, and it worked. Fortunately, as time went on, things smoothed over and all was well. Till this day, we have remained good friends and hope the best for each other.

I was already in high school now and was going to the other building in the other town. My best friend from second grade and I were still keeping in touch and still remained close, but it was not the same anymore. I would go watch her in track and go to their school dances and football games. I would also spend the night over there. This was where I met a really good-looking football player.

We all went to the dance after the game. He was seeing someone at the time. At the dance, while he was dancing with his girlfriend, our eyes locked and remained locked. We could not stop looking at each other. He was so good looking. At another time, we ran into each other at a wedding and *boom,* the same thing happened: our eyes locked, and the passion between us was tremendous.

We were both still very chicken to approach each other. Then one time, we met up at a park to finally talk. He asked me if I wanted to go out because he had broken up with his girlfriend. Oh, how I wanted to so badly but by that time, I was seeing my high school sweetheart. I still wonder about him today.

I noticed I had become the one to stay at other friends' homes now and not have friends come to my house. There were a few hang-out places we would go to. There was an arcade and a pizza restaurant. Another restaurant would hold dances that we went to, and sometimes we would go into a nearby state to a roller rink there. After basketball games, we always went to the pizza restaurant. It was and is still there today, and they have the best pizza ever! The local bar upstairs would hold dances every weekend for a while as well. At the arcade, I liked to play Pac-Man. I had a Rubik's Cube at the time as well. I could never figure that thing out. It ended up breaking.

When I was a freshman in high school, our neighbors next door in my grandpa's old house moved and new people moved in. They had a girl who was in the same grade as me. We all soon started hanging together and having fun as well. They buried me in the sand by the pond and took pictures of me with just my head sticking out. They buried me so deep I could not get out on my own. I could never do that today as I am very claustrophobic. She also had a leech from the pond attached to her inner thigh one time. That was a challenge to try and get off.

One weekend after the game, we were at the pizza restaurant and this senior guy was checking me out. We started flirting, he asked me out, and I said yes. He played the guitar and sang really well. It was so romantic. He swept me off my feet. He would play the guitar and sing to me. The Eagles were his favorite group. He sang "Desperado" to me. We saw each other for a while until I realized he had a couple other girls on the side besides me. I did not want that kind of relationship, so I broke it off. He would come over drunk and expect something, and when I said, "No, we were done," he sped off out the driveway mad.

He then went around to all the guys in high school, placing bets with them that if they asked me out, I would give them favors. A lot of guys asked me out and none of them got anywhere. I did not find out about the bet until later. It backfired on them. He went around spreading rumors, trying to ruin my reputation. It hurt really badly, but after a while, people saw the truth and I came out on top.

I started dating around, not tied down. I was going out with so many at one time that I had one over and one called me while that one was still over, and a third one was on his way over. I had to talk to the one on the phone without either knowing about the other, hanging up, and then get rid of the other guy before the next one came over. I was seeing three guys at once, but none of them got past a kiss. I pulled it off but I do not know how. I broke a few hearts, and felt really bad about it. Nothing was serious to me with any of them. It was only one date and maybe a kiss goodnight, but that was it.

Up until high school, I had a low self-esteem about myself and felt kind of nerdy. Once high school came, I began to blossom. I had a few good friends, but I never really fit into any one group. I talked with everyone and became popular. As well as being in track and choir, I was also in softball, volleyball, yearbook staff, and other clubs. In track, I met this really cute guy from the next state over who liked me. Unfortunately, that did not even go past a first date.

Now that I was older, I got to go on the semi with my brother and sometimes sister-in-law as well. One time, it was just my brother and I. We went to Jacksonville, Florida to a watermelon field. They had an assembly line right there in the field. They would pick the watermelon, tossing it to the next person until it reached the packer on the back of the semi.

The packer was built, beach blond, and tan. He was a surfer. He was very good looking. We hit it off. He went back with us to our hotel room to get a shower. He had told us he just got out of prison but did not say what he was in for. My brother left the room to go do something and left me alone with him while he was in the shower. I was kind of freaked out but all went well.

When he was done with his shower, he told me he took a shower with his clothes on and washed his clothes with a bar of soap. I thought that was very strange. I guess he did not have any money to do laundry. He did say I had the cutest feet and toes he had ever seen.

Out in the field, I had to go number 1 really badly, and my brother said to use a Dixie cup. It became an inside joke when I got back to school between a teacher of mine and I because I told him the story of being with my brother on the semi in Florida in a watermelon field having to go to the bathroom. I had a pretty good breast size developing and was called Miss Watermelons, and the keywords were watermelons and Dixie cups. We had so many watermelons left over from the semi that we had to sell some from our front yard.

I had been sick while on the semi and was taking erythromycin. It is an antibiotic. It did not agree with me, and I threw up in the semi in a towel. My brother had a bunk in his semi. It was really cool. I remember throwing ice cubes at him to keep him awake. The CB was neat too. His handle was the Entertainer. It was a fun time.

Before I started driving, during the last day of school one year in high school, a bunch of us decided to ride our bikes to school. I rode mine the seven miles from my home to the high school. This was the time for me to learn to drive as well. I started out with dad driving, and he let me steer. Then he let me drive while beside me. It was not so bad being on country roads. Passing a combine scared me to death, though. They are huge and take up the whole road. I never did learn how to drive stick and still do not know how. I have tried through the years but never really got it down. Then I took my test and passed.

My father bought me a used brown four-door car for my first car. I was coming home one day when a cow got out of its pasture. I was afraid I was going to hit it, so I swerved and went down into a ditch, and back up air born, flying through the air, into the middle of a field. My car was totaled, and I ended up with whiplash, but the cow was okay.

My dad took it well and got me another used car. This one was a light blue, two-door, with a white, vinyl top. I was going to school in the morning after it had snowed. I went to stop for a stop sign, but I was going too fast and slid until my car was facing the other direction and went right into a tree on the driver's side door of my car. It bent the whole door into the shape of the tree. I hit my head on the door window and had to wear glasses after that because it changed my vision. Well, car number two was totaled.

Now on high risk insurance, I told my father I would never drive again, but he made me get back behind the wheel again to face my fears. He did get me a third used little burgundy car, and I did not wreck that one. I guess third time is a charm. I also drove a grey car for a while. I did not go to the hospital for any of my accidents, and fortunately no one else was ever involved.

I did have the scare of my life one time while driving. There is this set of railroad tracks that was by my home. They sit up high and on an angle. There were no guardrails or signals at the time. My car at the time would like to stall out. I slowed down before going over the tracks, and as my car was going over the tracks, it stalled out. I looked, and a train was coming in the distance. I worked and worked to get my car to start, but it wouldn't. I was getting scared and didn't know what to do and wondered if I should jump out. Just then, with my first God experience, my car started just enough to get off the tracks and to stall back out, coasting down the hill away from the train as it went flying past. Angels were there that day.

Another scare of my life, but a totally different situation, was when I got done with track practice on a Friday after school. The school was holding a fish fry in the cafeteria. I was heading into the school, to the cafeteria from the track, carrying my gym bag. The halls were empty. A guy student there that I knew of came out of nowhere. He grabbed my gym bag and took off with it. Me, being naive, chased him to get it back.

He led me down into the industrial arts room. He got me cornered and then his eyes became really scary and he started to try and make out with me. I tried to push him away, and he became very aggressive and tried to start taking my clothes off. I kept trying to fight him off, but he was getting stronger and more forceful. Finally, somehow I broke free and started to run. I headed up the grey cement steps when he grabbed my ankle and pulled me back in. I kicked and fought enough to somehow get away again and ran like hell to the cafeteria where all the people were.

I found a male friend, an upper classman whom I trusted, and told him everything. I was crying and shaking. He went and got my gym bag back for me. I was so scared. Later, I found out that he did the same thing to a lot of other girls. He was so creepy. He would offer girls a ride home, get them on back roads, and attack them. God was with me that time as well.

As I grew older and made more and more friends, I would meet their families. I realized how different my family was from other families. My mom had a certain sound through the house when she walked. It was different than anyone else's. She walked on her heels. She never wore sandals or high heels. You see, I never saw my mother with toes. She was born with all ten toes but something took place before I was born.

My mom graduated from high school and soon married my father. They met on a double date and were originally with the other person, but hit it off so well that they ended up together. It was very soon after their marriage that she had my three brothers and then tragedy happened.

My mother snapped and was diagnosed with mental illness, paranoid schizophrenia, to be exact. Back then, they treated this illness differently. She was put in a mental institution about an hour away and was given shock treatments. She was there about seven years. My father was very committed. He would write her letters and would bring her home on weekends. My father's sister took care of raising my three brothers.

One time in the winter, my mother tried to escape from the institution. She was barefoot and froze her feet by the time they found her. They were able to save her feet, but she lost all her toes. I cannot even imagine how scared and lonely she may have felt and all she was going through. Her illness was never really discussed much with me in detail.

Growing up, it was always difficult to talk with my mother. I always went to my father for everything. There was always unconditional love from my mother. She just had odd behaviors. She did not like to take her medicine. I was never scared of my mother, and she never did anything harmful to me, herself, or anyone else in my lifetime. She may have been in her own little world at times, but she always, always, always, loved, cared, and adored me. She was always so proud of me. I loved my mom unconditionally.

This illness not only struck my mother, but her sister, my aunt, as well. My aunt was very religious. She would stay up all night in the bathtub, waiting for the Lord to come. She always thought it was the end of the world.

She would go into the town, on foot, near where she lived, in the middle of the night. She lived at home with grandma and grandpa. She would knock on people's doors, trying to wake everyone up to tell them Jesus was coming and that it was the end of the world and that they needed to wake up. My grandpa would have to go down to the police station and pick her up after the police would call him and tell him where she was. The poor lady finally, after living a very long life, got to go home to be with her Lord. She laid as a vegetable in a nursing home for years and years and years.

Unfortunately, some things are inherited to the next generation. This was the case in my family. It had struck again with my second brother. He had failed a couple grades in school and had to take them over. He did not date or go to prom. He went on his senior trip to New York, but became really homesick. He did graduate from high school and then soon after, it happened. He was struck with mental illness, paranoid schizophrenia, like my mother. He had worked a few jobs before being put on disability. He never got married or had children, and always lived at home with mom and dad.

I was really young when this happened. Even though there were almost twenty years between us, we seemed to be at the same age level as I grew up. We would play fox and rabbit together, as well as kick ball. We would play board games, cards, pick-up sticks, and jacks together.

When we went on the road with dad to sell his grease and oil, we would play road games, such as list the license plates or find a word that started with A-Z and the first one to finish would win. We played tractor and animal as well. You could only play on your side of the vehicle and whoever saw ten farm animals in a row would win. If you saw a tractor though, you would have to start over. We would have fun together. He was a big kid.

He did get his driver's license and was able to drive. He liked to collect postcards, pictures from calendars, and placemats from different restaurants. Dad collected some coins. My brother would sit in his bedroom and do his "figuring" as he would call it. That would consist of him taking a notebook and filling every sheet front and back with "1,000, 1,000, and 1,000." This was his millions, he would say.

He is so smart in some areas and other areas he lacks common sense. He was really good at checkers. He remembers the year people die and how old they were when they did. He knows all of the capitals to all of the states, but when it is cold outside, he does not know to put a coat on or take it off when it is too hot. Simple things like that, he does not understand. He needs verbal reminders such as pull up your pants when they fall down. My mom would always tell him to pull up his breeches. He needs reminded to take his medicine and to do his personal hygiene. He does not like change at all. It scares him a lot.

As a kid, he would tell me these stories. I knew they were not true, but he felt they were. He said he would see ghosts on the farm. He said he saw an owl with glasses on. He also said he was swallowed up by a snake and an angel made the snake puke him up and that is why he is still here today. It was not until I started to get older that I found myself seemingly older than him now and realized there was a difference.

By the time I reached high school, the third strike happened. They say it comes in threes. My youngest brother became hospitalized, and while there, his wife threw all of his belongings in the hospital parking lot and told him not to come back. My father went to pick him up with all of his belongings after being discharged from the hospital. He was diagnosed with bipolar psychotic disorder. He was in his thirties. His wife divorced him, and his son from his first marriage was adopted out. My father now really had his hands full.

I remember my brother when he came home just lied on the couch in a catatonic form. He would not move or even blink his eyes, like he was dead. It was so creepy. He would not eat, go to the bathroom, or respond in anyway. Eventually, he came out of that state, thank goodness. It was scary.

They say when you first experience the systems, your senses are all heightened. You can see and hear things on a different frequency than others. This was the case for both of my brothers. My older brother saw things, while my younger brother heard things. I know loud noises, too many people, or even television would bother my older brother. It becomes too much sensory overload for him. My younger brother being in the army would think that they were sending him secret messages through the static off a radio station or the humming of the refrigerator motor. He said he felt things coming from the power lines outside as well.

My freshman year of high school things really got real. My grandfather on my mom's side died. I do not believe my youngest brother had been diagnosed yet at that point. My older brother, who had the mental illness, had gone through his share of shock treatments like my mother. He also had taken different medications.

Being on medicine, a lot of times the body gets so used to it after being on it so long that it has to be changed. This can always be a challenge. Around this time, they had changed his medication, and it did not agree with him at all. He kept screaming, "Turn the burners off, turn the burners off. I'm on fire. I'm on fire." He ran out of the house, and my oldest brother, who was home at the time, had to run up the road to get him. My dad had tried to calm him down but could not.

Later, while I was at school, the police who I was great friends with, came and pulled me out of class and kept me in their police car. My brother had left the house on foot and told mom and dad that he was heading to the high school to kill me. They got my brother before he got to the high school. He was then hospitalized for over a month or so until they could get him on the right medication in a safe place for all of us.

As all of this took place, my father ended up having a massive heart attack. My dad was never sick except for being in the hospital once for a kidney stone. Our preacher drove us to the hospital where my father was taken. The doctors said he needed open heart surgery right away or he could die. He needed a triple bypass surgery. They explained the risk and that he could die during surgery as well.

I remember going into the hospital room where he laid and doing everything I could to hold back the tears. I was so scared. I went out in the hall and I begged God, saying, "Please don't take him now. Please let him see me get married and at least my first-born." I remember crying the whole way home in the backseat. I went through a whole box of Kleenex.

I remember when I got back, I had to go to a volleyball game. We were all on the bus and were listening to the songs "Eye of the Tiger" and "Physical." I remember staring out the window, over-whelmed with sadness and worry for my father and suddenly I felt very alone, even with all the other people on the bus around me. I did not feel anyone knew or even cared what I was going through or how I felt. I could not lose my dad. I just couldn't.

It was at this time that I rode on the back of my first love's moped to his house. I was feeling all alone and needed him at that time.

My father had the surgery and pulled through with flying col-ors. The Lord heard my prayer and answered me. He spared my dad's life. The doctor warned us that his personality might be different after this. A lot of patients with heart problems tend to go through personality changes, and it was true. Dad was not as patient as he had been in the past. He wore patches on his chest and took Valium. You could see his scar going all the way down the middle of his chest.

My brother got home from his hospital stay, and we all tried to resume our lives back to as normal as possible. While he was at the hospital, we would go visit him. He showed us how he played ping-pong while he was there. They helped get him straightened out, and he did really well after that. My mom and brother soon started taking a shot once a month of the same medicine (Prolixin) so they did not have to take the medicine daily any longer. This seemed to work really well for both of them for a really long time.

**

I was going into my sophomore year now and rebounding from the breakup of the guy trying to ruin my reputation. The rumor he was spreading was that I was crazy like the rest of my family. It was one thing to try and hurt me, but he brought my family into it and I was very protective of them and this hurt me more than ever. He was so mean to do that to me and my family, but in the long run, people knew the truth that I was not crazy, and I came out on top.

There was this senior guy who liked me. He was real tall and lanky. He had long arms and legs. He was really shy and had never gone out with girls before. He was awkward and nerdy. One day, he and his buddy put a note in my locker that said, "Hey Babe." I thought he was weird. We were in choir together and in a bookkeeping class together. Another one of his friends asked me if I would go out on a date with him.

I did not want to at first but I felt sorry for him and agreed to. For our first date, he picked me up in his little blue Subaru truck and we went to Pizza Hut and a movie. He was so shy, and I did all the talking. He made me order the pizza. I ordered the medium pan pizza with pepperoni and mushroom. Fortunately, he liked it. Then we went and saw the movie *Risky Business* with Tom Cruise dancing in his underwear to "Old Time Rock and Roll."

On our way home, I was doing all of the talking. He kept looking over at me and was swerving in the road, and so we got pulled over by the cops. They checked him to see if he was drinking. He was not, and they left him go. At that point, things became really awkward, and I did not talk anymore the rest of the ride home. I swore I would never go out with him again.

That same week, the same friend came up to me in choir and told me his friend wanted me to go to his house on the weekend and meet his parents. I said no. After that he left me alone.

Later in the year, a dance was coming up. I wanted to go but did not have a date. I knew he did not have a date, so I got up enough nerve to ask him in class if he wanted to go to the dance with me and he said yes. When we got there, my ex-boyfriend and his girlfriend were there and they were trying to make me feel bad, so we left.

When we got home, we stayed in the driveway and talked. I felt I owed him an explanation, and it turned into me confiding in him of my whole life story. Then I asked him if he wanted to be a couple. Both of us were really unsure how this was going to turn out, but he said yes. We saw each other at school and on weekends and talked on the phone the other times we were not together. He gave me his class ring on New Year's Day of 1984.

While dating my high school sweetheart, he bought me this white stuffed animal kitty sitting on a red heart pillow. It was small enough to put in my purse. I felt it was my good luck charm. Once, I lost my watch in my mom and dad's yard by the pond. I carried that kitty all over while looking for the watch and I eventually found it. I was a true believer after that. My kitty went everywhere with me, and I carried it in my purse to school, especially when I had to take a test or exam. I was superstitious. I broke a mirror once and was so scared of having bad luck for the next seven years. I would find four leaf clovers in the yard for good luck as well.

He was the water boy/manager for our basketball team. Our team was really good. We went to state. I attended all the games. I sat with the fans by the cheerleaders and the band, and cheered. I would gaze across the gym at my boyfriend. I was starting to fall in love. I felt secure in this relationship. I felt I had nothing to worry about with him having any other relationship with anyone else. He was not the type that girls would be all over him.

One time at a game, he gave me his keys to his truck and wanted me to start it. I felt so honored and walked out to the parking lot so happy and proud. I got in and went to start it and it rolled forward. I started to panic and put on the brakes. Then I just sat there holding the brakes, not moving my feet off them in fear of moving ahead further. His truck was a stick shift, and I had not learned how to drive a stick shift. Finally, I had help come and take over and all was well.

That scared the crap out of me. Here he trusted me with his vehicle, and I almost wrecked it in the parking lot trying to start the stupid thing.

Of course by now we had met each other's parents. His parents had never been divorced. I felt that was good. They had a nice home as well, and I felt that we were meant to be. We would spend a lot of fall and winter at his home and spring and summer at mine. We raked leaves at his home. He lived in a woods. In the winter, we went cross-country skiing. In the summer, we spent time at my mom and dad's pond, fishing, swimming, and spending time in our rowboat.

His parents took me in and started treating me as their own right away. He had two younger brothers, which I got along with as well. His parents would have me over for suppers. I would be in the kitchen with his mom. I would help her cook and do dishes and we would talk. She taught me how to peel potatoes with a knife, and I still can peel one without breaking the peel. I became really good at it. She taught me how to make strawberry freezer jam and home-made noodles. She was an amazing cook, and I got a lot of good recipes from her. We became really close.

She taught me how to go cut down corn stalks and tie them around the tree to decorate it for fall and putting the pumpkins around them. She would show me how to plant her flowers in her kettles outside in the spring. She planted inpatients and geraniums. She would take me with her when she bought them, too. She took me to pick strawberries in the summer.

We would celebrate holidays together. She even had a stocking at Christmas for me. They gave me lots of gifts at Christmas, which usually consisted of clothes. They celebrated my birthday with supper and a cake and gifts. We would go shopping and out to eat together. Other times, we just sat and watched TV and ate popcorn after supper. They had a little black poodle named Coco. His mom would give Coco baths in the kitchen sink.

I got my boyfriend a CB for Christmas. He got me an antique trunk. He also got me a calendar one year with a one hundred dollar bill laying on every month of the year, a twelve hundred dollar calendar. His mom was not happy about that at all. I paid my car off with it.

I took a family trip with them to the Smokey Mountains. We went to a Cincinnati Reds baseball game against the Los Angeles Dodgers. Pete Rose was with the Reds at that time and Tommy Lasorda was with the Dodgers. We went hiking to waterfalls in the mountains and went white water rafting at the Cherokee Indian Reservation in the Carolinas. My boyfriend and I sat in the back of the raft. I was hanging onto his leg for dear life. We both got knocked out of the raft. He got back in okay. His dad had to help me get back in. That was so scary.

Through the school years we remained high school sweethearts. We went to three proms together and all the dances. One of the proms theme songs was "We've Got Tonight," the song of my first love. My first love had dated others, some longer than others, but one particular girl he loved very much and was planning to marry was killed in an auto accident. This was extremely hard for him, and he reached out to me for comfort. My heart ached for him, and he wanted us to get back together. He said I remind him of her. I wanted to so badly but said no because I was in this relationship already.

My boyfriend and I were in love. I loved him so much. We would give each other body rubs. He would have me file his fingernails, which I found odd but did it anyways. He graduated from high school and went to college for auto-diesel mechanic. He roomed with a high school friend. His roommate's girlfriend and I would go down and visit them. We would go to the mall. The girlfriend and I became close friends and our friendship has still remained to this day. Even though I have moved, we keep in contact with each other.

One thing I started to notice is that he and his family did not go to church. I started questioning his beliefs. When I asked him about it, he said he believes there is heaven and hell and God and Satan, but God already knows and has chosen for him where he will go when he dies and he does not have a choice in the matter and is not going to worry about it. This bothered me, but I was young and naive and thought that should not be a problem.

Being it his senior year in high school when we met, he wanted to live it up, and drinking beer with his buddies was the thing to do. He would chew chewing tobacco as well. He also loved to go hunting.

He would go home so drunk and he would need to go to the bathroom and did not know where he was, so he would try and pee on chairs. His mom would wake up and stop him and walk him to the bathroom. It would make her angry. Her house was spotless and she had to have everything perfect at all times, but they also drank, so drinking was normal in their household. This was very different for me because we did not drink in our household. The drinking followed him into college of course. I once again blew this behavior off, thinking it was just a stage.

As I got closer to the family, I started seeing a different side to his mom in particular. She would get mad at her husband and would not talk to him for days or even weeks at a time. This was so abnormal for me. I started to learn she was very unhappy inside. She loved to gossip, criticize, and put everyone and everything around her down.

She was very obsessive with her housework. She would have to go around the kitchen table and center each chair just right and center the phone on the wall just right. I started feeling that she could not be trusted fully. I felt she was judging me as she did everyone else and that I was not good enough. Being raised with so much unconditional love, I did not understand why she was acting this way towards me when I thought we were getting along great.

I guess she thought we were getting too close before he went off to college and she wanted him to enjoy his senior year with his friends and not be tied down, and did not want me to ruin his future. I did not understand this at the time and became very hurt by the way she started treating me. She had made comments to me to make me feel she was trying to convince her son that drinking and his friends were more important than me.

I started turning a lot of guys' heads, even the cute and popular ones. There was one guy who really liked me. While playing softball, I thought the lady umpire was his mom. I admired her. I tried to like him before, but it just was not there for me. Later, I found out that the lady umpire was not his mom, but my boyfriend's aunt. This made me even happier to be with him.

This guy still liked me, and it bothered my boyfriend. It bothered him so much that after drinking on a weekend, the two met up to have a fist fight about it. My boyfriend ended up with a black eye and a fat lip. He joined karate after that. He stayed with it until he could break a board. I went to some of his meets.

It was my junior year in high school now, and my self-esteem was higher than ever. I had blossomed into an attractive girl. I was bubbly and positive, and I talked to everyone. I never had a single best friend at this time, and I never joined a particular clique. I was a loner, so to speak. I got along with everyone, the nerds and the popular crowd as well.

It was getting close to homecoming, and the students had to vote for the homecoming court. Each grade voted for who they wanted on the court. They announced this over the speakers during school. The top four people for each class were announced. When my name was called, I almost fell out of my chair. I was shocked. I was one of the top four! I was so overwhelmed and full of joy and so proud of myself. Growing up feeling like a nerd, this was the farthest thing from my mind. After announcing the names, we all had to vote again from the top four names. I felt great just being in the top four. I did not feel I would get it because there were two other girls I felt were more popular than me. After the voting took place, they announced the winners.

"For the junior class," they went to announce, me being on the edge of my seat, as they continued talking on the intercom. I waited to hear the name. Then they said it. They called my name. They called my name? Did they really call my name? They did! Oh my gosh, oh my gosh, oh my gosh! I could not believe it! A dream all girls wish for, and it happened to me. It was way beyond my wildest dreams. I was so overwhelmed with joy inside, but was working so hard to hold it in and stay humble. Wow, wow, wow, wow! "Way to go," I told myself. "You did it."

Now, the next challenge was ahead. I needed to have my dad walk me into the gym in front of a whole crowd of people during half time of the basketball game. He did not like big crowds of people and he was nervous. He agreed to do it, but was not happy about it. He was chewing gum to calm him down. I was so happy and proud he was there with me. You see, my parents did not attend any of my school activities. Dad had too many responsibilities of taking care of everybody, so I never experienced that kind of support like other children did. I had learned to accept it early on and understood the circumstances. It was still not easy.

It was hard for me to enjoy this moment because I was worried about my dad, I was nervous as all get out, and I knew my boyfriend's parents were in the audience. I felt they were judging me and I was still not good enough. In the back of my mind, I wondered if I got voted because people really liked me or if I was just voted for as a big joke. I chose to believe the first reason. I was not letting my low self-esteem from my past get into my head and believe the second reason. I chose to ignore my doubts and not let that ruin my moment. I had a hard time believing that a genuine good thing could happen to me. I wore the same dress that I wore to prom. It was pink. I wore it to two of my proms as well. For my senior prom, I bought a different dress. Why I did not get a special dress for this special occasion, I have no idea.

I saw the band Loverboy and Kiss without their makeup on. Later on in life, I had the opportunities to see a whole bunch of singers, including Diamond Rio, Whitney Houston, John Melloncamp, Huey Lewis and the News, Rick Springfield, Shania Twain, Styx, REO Speedwagon, Meatloaf, Elton John, Barry Manilow, Glee, and Idina Menzel. I also saw *Phantom of the Opera* and *Wicked* as well as other musicals and plays.

I had been invited when I was younger to go see Rick Springfield at the fair with a friend and didn't go. I fortunately saw him years later.

I had a friend who was going with a group of people to see Huey Lewis and the News. I was still in high school, and they had no way to get there, so they asked to use my car, but I was not invited to go. I let them use my car, but I was so upset that I couldn't go, too. Years later, however, I got to see him, too. Another friend borrowed my car as well. Her father died and needed it for the funeral. I was a trusting person, with other people, to use my car, with me not being along. Luckily, my car came back in one piece both times.

During my senior year, I went with my boyfriend to a Motley Crue concert. My boyfriend caught the drumstick and put it down his pants. He was a huge fan.

That night when I got back, I had to finish packing for my senior trip to Florida. We went to the Wet 'n Wild water park. It was chilly. We went to Disney, Daytona Beach, and the NASA space center. I saw an alligator at the NASA space center on an island in a pond. It was in the open and there was no fence or other device that could restrict it from getting out. I was not aware that the sun was much hotter in Florida compared to up north. My lips, chin, and mouth got burned pretty bad and bubbled on the surface. It took a long time to heal.

My friend's mom lived down there, and they had not seen each other in a while, so they wanted to spend time alone together. I felt like an outsider, so I left them in Disney and walked around by myself until I caught up to a group of other girls I knew to hang with. My friend and I were rooming together with two other girls. After my friend saw her mom, she was moody with me, so I kept my distance as much as possible. I hung with the guys a lot and another girl friend. My friend and I resumed our close friendship after the tension passed for many years. We had been close friends since junior high school. I called her Burt and she called me Ernie. I miss her and think of her often. She became my hairdresser many years later. Having our paths cross again was so awesome, and I cherish that and her so much.

Coming back from the trip, everyone had people welcoming them home. Our bus pulled into the school parking lot. We all got off, and everyone went with their rides home. There was no one there to pick me up. Not my boyfriend, not my parents, no one. I had to call someone to come and get me. My brother came and picked me up. I was so embarrassed, humiliated, hurt, and angry that no one missed me enough to come and get me or welcomed me home. When I got home, I went straight to my room and locked the door. I walked past everyone and did not say a word. They did not say a word either. Why weren't they glad I was home, and why didn't they want to know about my trip, and where the heck was my boyfriend? I was so angry with them all.

On my senior year, I lost my last living grandparent, my maternal grandmother. Get-togethers for holidays were never the same again. While digging through a family tree, I discovered how history had kept repeating itself. On my father's side, my grandpa's mother died when my grandpa was two years old. Then my grandma died when I was two years old. Then my father died when my daughter was two years old. They say it goes in threes. The three is up, so that better be the end of that.

My high school sweetheart and I started hanging around another couple all the time. The guy was actually my distant cousin. We would go on double dates, out to eat, to the bars, and out dancing. Sometimes we would just play cards at the other couple's place. We all liked country music.

I had become very close with one of my high school teachers. I would go to her house. We made buckeyes and exchanged gifts at Christmas. I was a server in her wedding, and we remembered each other on birthdays.

Besides getting junior attendant for homecoming, I also received a scholarship my senior year for college. That was another huge dream that I never expected and was so proud of. Our last choir concert, during my senior year, we received awards. At this time, I missed this event because I was in the hospital with a kidney infection. I was so disappointed that I couldn't go. My teacher came to the hospital to give me my award. That was a huge surprise.

When I sent out invitations for my graduation party, I forgot to invite one of my neighbors. They still came and I felt so bad that I didn't send them one. It bothered me so badly that I had a nightmare that they committed suicide because of it. Well, not that long after my dream, another neighbor down the road did commit suicide. That really freaked me out. This was the first of many incidents like this to happen to me. Coincidence, intuition, ESP, or from God, I was to have many more situations like this in my life.

As I had my challenges in high school now, my best friend from second grade was having her share as well. She ended up in an abusive relationship with a guy. It changed her so drastically, and she is still not the same to this day.

***

Graduating from High School

We had a relatively small graduating class of around fifty. I just missed the top 10% of the class with my GPA. I was eleventh in the class. We had our graduation outside in front of the high school. It was a beautiful sunny day. I was so glad. I was so worried it would rain and have to be held inside and I wanted it to be outside. I had prayed about it and it was perfect.

The senior choir sang. I was among them. I do miss choir. Our instructor was the best. We would always come home from state competitions with awards. They gave us scores like the Olympics. The best you could score was one, and we got that every year. We were awesome.

The girls' caps and gowns were white and the guys' were black. Our colors were black, white, and red.

I remember marching out of the building to the music to take our spot up front by the speaker. I was so nervous and excited. I was in the front line at the end.

After the ceremony, we got in a line along the sidewalk and threw up our caps. People came through to see us. My oldest brother was there, and I was so excited about that. I had a picture taken with him.

Afterward, we had a party at my mom and dad's. I had pictures taken with several different people, including my boyfriend, my parents, my best friend from second grade, and my best friend's mom. I also had my picture taken next to my pine tree I planted in second grade, with my cap and gown on. The tree was much taller than me then. That tree is still there today. My mom never drank and my boyfriend had beer there, so my mom picked up a can of beer and guzzled it. This was the beer I was referring to earlier in my story with my mother. We all thought that was hilarious. I also got a suitcase and a huge body towel with my name on it in white thread. It was peach. I had a cake of course, and we all had a really nice time. I still have my towel.

A couple years after graduating high school, the week of November 22, 1988 to be exact, a very good friend that I graduated with was in a car accident on her way home from college. It was around her birthday, and she wanted to rent a white limo to ride around in for her birthday. She was coming home to see her family. The accident was where someone ran a stop sign and crashed into her. It was raining. There was a curve and an overpass above her where it took place. She was knocked out and sent to the hospital. Her brain had started to swell, and they had to shave her head to do what they could to try and relieve the pressure of the swelling.

She was in a quartet. The other three girls that sang with her were all sisters. Most of them went to the hospital and sang to her in her room in hopes it would wake her up but to no success. Eventually, within a few days, the family had to make that dreaded decision to pull the plug. They did, and she did not make it. The three sisters all decided to sing at her funeral. Before the funeral, I was driving past the sisters' home on my way home, and all of a sudden, I felt a very heavy heart for them. I thought it was just the fact that they would be singing at the funeral and it was going to be hard for them. When I got home, I found out their oldest brother was also killed in a car accident. This was such a tragedy in just a few days for our small community.

Almost everyone came to both services. The three sisters ended up singing at both funerals. How they did this, I will never know. It was God helping them to get through it. The friend's funeral was so hard on her family. She was the only girl and the youngest. Her boyfriend and all her brothers carried the casket. Her father had gotten white limos for the funeral since she didn't get them for her birthday. The brothers had a very hard time carrying the casket. They had to stop on the cement stairs outside the church because the one brother was taking the loss so hard he literally collapsed into tears. The rest of the brothers and boyfriend stood completely still until the brother could collect himself enough to continue down the steps. It was the hardest thing to watch. It broke your heart. Then that same week, we all went to the other funeral for the three girls' brother.

I had gone on a date with him once. We went to a drive-in theater and watched *Psycho.* We went to a restaurant and had a grilled cheese sandwich like in the movie.

The family's strong faith saw them through. The song "Oh, Baby, Baby, It's a Wild World" was popular on the radio and was played around this time, and whenever I hear that song today, it takes me back to this week. There were so many young people who were from that school or neighbors or just in the next town over that died after this. There were a lot of car accidents and a couple that were killed by a train. Some were also gun accidents and a few died from illnesses.

A couple of years after this week of tragedy, a senior was killed in a car accident, just before his graduation. He had gone on the senior trip and was the only one that was not in the class picture on the trip. He missed it somehow. It was like a prediction almost. His mother took it very, very hard. They ended up moving eventually to be able to try and get on with their lives. That was another really hard one.

There was a car accident that killed another person from the next town over the year I graduated. My best friend went to that school and graduated that year too. I went to her graduation. It was a junior attendant that was killed, and they left a blank chair for where that person was supposed to sit. It was in the gym, but they could open the one end to the outdoors. It was open that day, and when they announced the person who died and to have remembrance for that person, a bird flew in and kept circling the empty chair and then flew back out. It was the weirdest thing.

When my boyfriend graduated from college, I went with his family and we all went out to eat afterward. His first job after graduation was working as an auto-diesel mechanic on school buses. He then got hired where his father always worked. It was a factory, working second shift, in maintenance. When a machine broke down, he had to fix it. He drove a little blue Subaru pickup truck.

These were my junior high and high school years.

Chapter 14

JOBS AND COLLEGE DAYS

I babysat at a few homes. One family on weekends, another family a mile over or so. I went to babysit here right after school my senior year. One day while babysitting, I had the television on and it was broadcasting the space shuttle taking off into space. A lot of astronauts were on board, as well as a female teacher. It was called the *Challenger*. I was watching the countdown to take off. It left the launch pad, and once in the air, it all of a sudden exploded right before everyone's eyes. Debris went everywhere into the ocean. When they waved to everyone before getting on board, that was their last wave good-bye. Everyone who was on board died. It was a very sad moment in time. One of which you remember where you were and what you were doing when it happened. That was in 1986.

I also babysat for the neighbor down the road. Another job I had was working at the local rest stop. I cooked, ran the gift shop, and cleaned the dreaded stainless steel restrooms. How people would get toilet paper all over the floor was simply amazing. Do people do this at home? It was a huge pet peeve of mine. I hated that part of the job. Busloads of people would come in, and we would be busy behind the grill, serving people. I learned to butter the buns and put them on the grill before putting the hamburger on it.

Once I got to college, I worked part time for an accounting teacher. I was going to college full time at the local community college and was commuting. I was working on getting a nine-month certificate in word processing. It was a new program and was to be the same as an associate degree, just done faster. I had all business classes: accounting, transcription, typing, shorthand, adding machine, and communication. It was so much different than high school. It was in an atmosphere as you were on the job but learning. I felt so grown-up and so excited. All those years of playing secretary and now there it was, the real thing. I couldn't be any happier.

I was able to get grants with my scholarship, so I had no college debt to pay. I had a close friend from high school who was taking the same classes as me. I was close to her mom also since I had spent the night at her house many times. Her mom was a police officer and was there for me throughout several incidents in my life. They are both very dear friends to me. I rode with my friend one winter. We ended up sliding on the snow into a ditch. We were banged up but okay. We became friends with another girl as well who had the same classes.

Accounting was so hard because you had this packet, and the homework was just an extension of what was already done. You make any error, and it would mess everything up the whole way through. I spent many of overnights trying to get it right and never succeeded. My communication teacher was a hard grader. Cs to him were As. I got mostly Cs, maybe a couple of Bs, and one A-. That paper was to be about details. I talked about being in love throughout the four seasons. I used a lot of details. I saved that paper. My only A in the class. Transcription was new that year and the teacher didn't have the bugs worked out and everyone was struggling in the class.

When it got close to graduating, I was concerned of what I was getting in transcription, so I stayed after class and asked the teacher my grade. It was not good. It would have kept me from graduating. I begged her to see if there was anything I could do to bring my grade up. She had me do some things to hand in and grade, and I did them all and did not leave that classroom until she graded them all in front of me and until my grade was up enough to graduate. I had done this just in time as well. I said something to my other two friends, and they blew it off; otherwise, all my grades in all my other classes were good.

On graduation, we all walked with our caps and gowns on. My cap and gown were grey. We had the ceremony outside. At the time, the college broke ground at graduation to build on and the name changed. I received my nine-month certificate. My one friend did not, and she was devastated. She didn't follow up with the transcription class like I did, and it bit her in the butt. I felt bad for her. I believe she did end up finishing okay. I don't remember for sure though.

My first job after college was working for an agency called Coin. I was to do data entry for them. They were responsible for all the information to be updated on the computers for all of the colleges in the United States. It was my job to get the new information typed into the computer. The place I worked was held in the offices where they sold ice cream. They made ice cream there, and it was sold locally to stores. They had a parlor there. My parents took me there when I was young. They had a pet monkey in a diaper. I used to love going there to see the monkey and have ice cream.

Nearby, a town had a place set up like an old-time village. It was always a fun place to go. It was a village with little buildings you could tour that took you back in time. There was a blacksmith shop, an old railroad station, doctor's office, barbershop, candy store (I loved the candy sticks!), a place that does blown glass, a museum, a barn with animals, a train, a barn that is a restaurant (They had such good home-cooked food buffet style.), a hotel, and a bakery, and so much more. We would go on field trips there too.

We also went to a similar place but on a much larger scale the state next to us. We went both places as a family and on field trips with the school. When I went with the school to the next state from us, we stayed the night there and slept in our sleeping bags on the museum floor. I was so scared because there were mummies in there, and I was afraid they would come to life. I was so homesick.

When I was younger, whenever we had to perform at school for a certain program and it got dark out, I would be so nervous and would get a stomachache and wouldn't want to go. I finally outgrew that. I would almost panic and cry. It was not fun. I'm so glad I got past that.

***

It was now 1987. After working for Coin, which was only a temporary job, I took my resumes around to places. I ended up getting an interview at a factory in a local town. They made drill bits there. I remember the man who interviewed me. He resembled Tom Selleck from the TV show *Magnum, P.I.* He had the mustache too. I ended up getting the job. It was full time, first shift (which was eight to five, with an hour lunch break), Monday through Friday, and an office job.

There was a receptionist who sat in a room off the really big room with partitions. It was enclosed with a glass window that led out to the lobby and front door. She had a long built-in desk with a really, really huge switchboard. She wore a headset and answered all the phone calls. It would get so busy. She would answer, put everyone on hold, go back to the first caller, transfer it, and onto the next person on hold. She was really fast and good at it. She greeted people that came in and did some filing and other jobs that needed done that she could do at her desk. She was dating one of the salesmen, and they ended up getting married. They loved to downhill ski. I thought they were so romantic. There were other couples that worked there that were married as well.

They had lots of customers, and each customer had their own folder. Each folder was filed. We had rows and rows of files, and that is where I started out. I was to file the folders that were done and pull out the ones they needed. Sometimes a customer may have ended up with two or more folders because companies may have merged or something, and we would have to combine them.

They would have me call back quotes to the customers as well. I learned a lot about drill bits. Some had carbide tips. It made them stronger. I learned about flutes. That is the spiral of the drill bit. They would come in different sizes and measurements between each flute or spiral and depth. We had really big accounts like Boeing aircraft. Their folders were called blankets, and they were really thick.

I eventually worked my way up to the order desk. I did run some copies and send faxes as well. At the order desk, I got my own desk in my own partition in that big room shared by others. Along the one wall with the front windows were all the sales people. My partition was next to the quote desk and the files and the receptionist.

Accounting was along the back wall, while the engineers were along the far wall near the vice-president's office. Customer service was more in the middle as well as the manager who was my boss. She did scheduling, hiring and firing, and our paychecks. She helped when people got behind or filled in when someone was absent. The human resources department was located in another part of the building. They took care of our insurance benefits back then.

My desk was where it all began. I got the mail, the orders from the customers that came in. I would have to look up the customers on the computer and the type of drill bit they were ordering. This would let me know the exact folder number they had. I would write all the folder numbers down on the orders. After that was done, I would have to go to the files and find them and take them back to my desk. I had to correct any errors I found or combine folders if there were more than one by accident. Once that was done and any quotes needed done, I had to give them to the office next to me so they could do the quotes. Other ones that were ready to go on, I had to take to the engineer's department and they had to draw up blueprints for the certain drill bits. We would get tons of orders and were really busy.

One day, the guy who interviewed me, was in the same row of files as I was. He came over to me and intentionally grabbed my breast. Little did I know, during a company picnic, he had done similar things to other women. He ended up resigning because of the sexual harassment. Later in life, I had experienced a few more incidents like this with other men outside of the workplace. I really liked my job and all the people I worked with besides the guy who grabbed me. I eventually got to train people on my desk. I became very good friends with a couple of these people, one especially that I still keep in contact with today. One person I trained called me Weenie, and I called her Chuck. I would go to her house a lot, and we would hang out. She was really talented and could paint pictures on my fingernails by hand with a really tiny brush. We got along great.

My boss called me snot-nosed kid because I was the youngest of the bunch and the new kid on the block, so to speak. Another older lady that worked there along time was called Mother McKenzie. We would have lunch together and awesome Christmas parties. They became very supportive and protective of me and really became like family to me.

We would all get together after work on Friday evenings and go out to eat. We had a blast. Traveling to the restaurant, we would moon people out the windows of the vehicles and do a Chinese fire drill and laugh, laugh, laugh. Once we would get to the restaurant we would be the loudest table and we would laugh and get everyone else in the restaurant to join in. We all knew how to party and have a great time.

On my twenty-first birthday, they were determined to get me drunk. I had never drank before. We were on our way to a bar after work, and they had me drink a wine cooler. Once we were at the bar, they ordered me a sex on the beach, a screaming orgasm, a strawberry daiquiri, and a piña colada. They ended up tying a balloon to my belt loop, and it bounced around everywhere I went. Then they gave me five whiskey slammers. After that, I was spinning. They succeeded. I was drunk. I needed to go pee and couldn't walk to the bathroom, so I had a person on both sides of me trying to walk me there. The bathrooms were full, and I thought I was going to be sick, so we headed to the parking lot for some air.

It was broad daylight out, and I started leaning on cars in the parking lot, laughing hysterically at the license plates for no reason at all. The people with me were laughing because I was laughing so hard. I was wearing a jean mini skirt. I ended up peeing down my leg because I was laughing so hard. I finally got to the restroom. My boss was in there drunk too, and we were both laughing hysterically. She couldn't pull her pants up and button them because she was so drunk. I never threw up, thank goodness. That was the only time I had ever been drunk like that.

My jobs and college days were fun and exciting.

Chapter 15

ENGAGEMENT AND WEDDING

My high school sweetheart and I were still dating. It was 1988 in October on sweetest day when he came over to my house to see me. He came to my bedroom, handed me a dozen roses, and then laid on my bed, where he buried his head in my pillow. I bend down to smell the roses, which were so pretty and such a nice surprise, to find a diamond ring inside one of the roses. I couldn't believe my eyes! Was this for real? It was beautiful! I didn't know what to say! He was peeking over the pillow to see my reaction. I took the ring out of the rose and looked at it. I asked him if that was what I thought it was, and he said, "Yes. What do you think?" I said yes and put it on and hugged him really hard. We set the date for August 19, 1989. We had engagement pictures taken and put in the newspaper. I was twenty-one years old when I got married. He was twenty-two.

Well, I had a lot of planning to start doing now. I decided to go with a light lavender for the color of the wedding. We ended up with four bridesmaids and four groomsmen. The guys wore grey tuxes, while we were both in white. The girls wore the lavender dresses. I had my sister-in-law and her one daughter in the wedding. She had two daughters, and I would have had both but she wasn't around at the time. My best friend from second grade was my maid of honor, and I had another friend as the bridesmaid.

I also wanted to ask another friend. She was the one who took my car to see Huey Lewis and the News with a bunch of friends. She had planned a wedding for herself and asked people to be in the wedding. They ordered their dresses and put money down on them. Then she backed out of the wedding, but none of the girls got their money back. The one friend I had, who was in my wedding, was one who didn't like this and didn't want her in my wedding. My fiancé didn't want her in our wedding either, so to keep the peace, I didn't ask her. I found out really fast that the close friends I did have in the wedding were either one-sided and used me and wanted me there for them but didn't want to be there for me. The ones that were there for me wanted to control everything. I was pretty much doomed.

My fiancé had his two brothers, cousin, and best friend (the best man), as his groomsmen. His best man and one of my bridesmaids were already married to each other. I was a server at their wedding, and my fiancé was a groomsman in their wedding. I was so disappointed because I wanted to be a bridesmaid.

As the year flew by and dress fittings, showers, and planning a bachelorette party were happening, my maid of honor was nowhere around to do these responsibilities. She was a flight attendant and couldn't get off work. She worked out of Las Vegas. She disappointed the other friend who was married to the best man, so she did all of the arrangements. I made her the matron of honor instead. I don't think my best friend liked that very much, but she was not there for me. That was the bottom line.

I had five showers. My mom went to some but couldn't make it to all of them. She tripped and fell in my kitchen and broke her arm. My aunt threw a kitchen shower, and the neighbors came and gave me recipes and helpful household hints on note cards. I had to wear an apron, sweep with a broom, answer the phone, and iron all at the same time. It was a game we played. I got dishtowels and measuring spoons and things like that.

The bridesmaid threw a shower. My fiancé's paternal aunt threw a shower, and his maternal aunt threw one as well. One was a bedroom shower and the other was a bathroom shower. The people I worked with also threw me a shower as well.

I had to get the dress ordered, the cake ordered, the flowers ordered, the photographer, the video, the church, the preachers, the organist, the music, the reception hall, the caterer, the DJ, and get the decorations. Also, I had to get the guest book and the person assigned to oversee it, the flower girl, ring bearer, the people to pass out the rice, and the vehicle. I had so many things to do. I also had to order the invitations and thank-yous as well. I rented heart-shaped candelabras. Like my scrapbook from high school, I kept a scrapbook for the wedding as well. I had to order the cake top, knife and server, pillow, wine glasses, and the unity candle. So many things to think about.

My best friend disappointed me so badly that she was not there for me during all of this planning for the wedding. It really hurt my feelings, but I forgave her and moved on. She was not interested in having me and my wedding be a priority in her life. I knew she was working, but she could have worked around it if she really wanted to a little bit.

My fiancé bought a ranch-style home with his parents' involvement and pretty much chose to keep me out of any of the decision-making. He rented it out for a year until we got married and then we were to move into it together. We had gone and bought furniture together and stored it until the renters moved out. The couch and chair were tan and were like big, overstuffed pillows. They were so comfortable. Even the arms of the furniture were cushy.

When I went shopping for my dress, my mom, fiancé's mom, and my bridesmaid went. I had seen this one dress and fell in love with it. I tried it on and loved it. However, my fiancé's mom wanted me to keep looking. I tried on all of the dresses that she wanted me to wear. There was one dress I tried on that she loved and wanted me to get instead of the one I loved. It looked nice on me, and I did like it, but I was not in love with it like I was with the other one. I didn't know how to say no to her, so I ended up buying the dress she wanted. I had taken a picture of me in both dresses.

I left there and went home feeling so miserable inside. I was so unhappy. I wanted the other dress so badly. I called the store, but they didn't have the dress I wanted. Fortunately, they could order it and put some of the money down on it that went on the other dress that I already paid for. I lost out on some money, but I was so happy and relieved with my decision. This was *my* wedding day, and

I should be allowed to get what I wanted. When my fiancé's mom found out, she was not happy about it. I felt bad that she was upset, but I had to stand up for myself and get what I wanted.

I was getting very upset that my soon-to-be mother-in-law was controlling everything and that I didn't have the freedom to make any decisions or choices of my own. My soon-to-be brother-in-law's girlfriend was around me when I let the anger get the best of me. I had said, "Once we are married, she better be careful or she is going to lose a son." She later went back and told my soon to be mother-in-law even though it was supposed to be confidential. It was something I said out of anger and frustration and regretted saying it after I did.

We had to go for my bachelorette party, and my mother-in-law was furious. She was one to hold a grudge forever and did not believe in talking things out or seeing the whole picture, let alone apologizing and forgiving. She was an expert at the silent treatment. That is what she always did when she got mad, even to her husband. She felt that talking and communicating was fighting and she didn't fight. She didn't want to communicate because she thought she was always right. She did not know how to communicate properly. Her behavior was very abusive and toxic.

My bachelorette party was very awkward and not very fun for me. We went to a bar with strippers I think. I don't really remember. I just remember having a lousy time because of the drama with my mother-in-law. Naturally, this girlfriend was now "buddy, buddy" with my mother-in-law.

The day before the wedding, we had the rehearsal and my soon to be mother-in-law was giving me the silent treatment, even more now than ever. We all ate at a restaurant together after we practiced at the church. I was so miserable and couldn't enjoy anything because of her. I was so angry at the girlfriend for running her mouth like she did. Those words I said were not meant for my mother-in-law to hear. The girlfriend was nothing but a little troublemaker, ruining a special time for all of us. It sure is funny that after the wedding and creating chaos, she dumped my brother-in-law and moved on, but only after the damage was done.

My mother-in-law had gotten into a fight with her own sister. Her sister had seen my side of things and tried to point out to her what she was doing was wrong, but she didn't listen to any of it and chose to stop talking to her as well. I started to see she didn't like her sister-in-law as well. She just wanted to control everyone's lives, and when she couldn't, she became very angry at everyone.

At the dinner, I gave all the girls in the wedding their gifts and necklaces to wear. My matron of honor gave me lingerie and a mini photo album with instant pictures from the rehearsal to take with us on the honeymoon. After the dinner was over, we all went home. My best friend came to my house and stayed the night one last time with me in my childhood bedroom. She talked some to her boyfriend on the phone while I went over my lists. I was making sure I had everything around for the next day. I was also packing for the honeymoon.

My head was spinning. I didn't want to forget anything. I could hear my mom talking to my dad in their bedroom. Their room was next to mine. She was crying and saying that I can't marry him. My dad kept saying she had to let me go. My friend got tired and fell asleep, but I just couldn't sleep at all. I was just too wound up. I just kept going over my list, making sure I didn't forget anything. I never did go to sleep.

When daylight hit, I took a shower. That morning, when my hair was still wet, the receptionist I worked with brought my wedding gift to the house from all of my co-workers. It was a microwave. I had gotten a wooden calendar as well, and my friend painted different holidays on the plain wooden tiles for me.

It was now the big day, and we went to the church. I had my hair done at home first, but I took the dress to the church and changed there. My hair was finished some at the church, and I didn't wear a lot of makeup, only mascara and light lipstick gloss. My hair was done like the eighties style puff, a big hairdo, all curled back around the whole head and on top. I had a veil with a headpiece. The veil went down the back of my dress to just below my butt. The veil was also divided to come over the top of my head to cover my face as I walked down the aisle.

My dress was satin with lace sleeves that were long and puffy at the shoulders with pearls. It was a V-neck with scallops with lace, pearls, and sequins on the bodice. The skirt of the dress had lace near the bottom, and it was trimmed the whole way around the bottom with lacy scallops. I had fluffy netting on my butt. Satin buttons were down my back with netting. The train was long with the lace design on it as well. I wore white silk flat ballerina shoes. I also wore pearl drop earrings that matched.

The girls were taught how to bustle my train up after the wedding. It was tuck, tuck, tuck, and fluff, fluff, fluff. We got pictures taken before the wedding as much as we could without my soon-to-be husband and me seeing each other. The rest of the pictures with us together were taken after the wedding.

Things were going along smoothly until the florist said she couldn't get the girls' heart baskets made out of grape vines that they were each going to carry. She ended up getting heart wreaths made out of grape vine instead for them to carry. I was upset at first, but it worked out. My matron of honor kept calming me down.

My mom and I had a picture taken together when she was fixing my veil. My father and I had a picture taken together where he put a penny in my shoe. I had my "something old, something new, something borrowed, something blue." My dress was new, my pearl necklace was old since it was my grandmother's, I borrowed a handkerchief, and wore a blue garter.

My bouquet of flowers had a penny taped to the back of the handle and my flowers were huge. They were really pretty but very, very heavy to carry. My hand was so sweaty and clammy, and I had a hard time hanging on to the flowers. My hands kept slipping. We had both moms light our single candles. The florist lit our unity candle before the wedding and blew it out because they said it is harder to light a new wick.

I had both my parents walk me down the aisle. I remember being in the hall getting ready to enter the sanctuary with both parents by my side. I was so nervous! It seemed so unreal that this day had come. When we got to the front, my dad lifted my veil over my head and gave me away. During rehearsal, he was so afraid he would say it wrong the day of the wedding, so he wrote it on his hand to remember.

"Who gives this woman in marriage to this man?" He wrote on his hand, "Her mother and I." He did wonderful and said everything correctly.

Things were going along beautifully and then it was time to light our unity candle. We went to light it, and no matter how hard we tried, it would not light. The florist burned the wick down so short that it wouldn't light. We couldn't get it to light, and through the whole song, my husband was trying to calm me down because I was getting very upset. We never got it lit, and we went back down to the keeling bench. I was so devastated. I felt this was a sure sign of something bad.

After the wedding, my new father-in-law saw how upset I was. He carved out some wax in order to get the candle to light for the pictures afterward. He was successful in getting it to light. I was grateful to him for this and for him trying to make me feel better, but even though it finally lit, I still felt a heaviness about it not lighting during the wedding. The unity candle was a symbol to become one and blessed by the Lord, and I felt that now it was not blessed or that we would not become one.

As we were getting the pictures taken, my mother-in-law refused to smile in any of the pictures and still refused to speak to me at all. In the receiving line after the wedding, even though she was mad at her sister, she hugged her sister tight, crying, and talking with her, but she wouldn't even acknowledge me. I was so upset. It was hard to try and not let it ruin my special day. I just wanted us to make amends and get along.

I felt there was this curse on our unity candle. Things went well at the reception, and I loosened up a little more and started to have fun, regardless of the unity candle and my mother-in-law. After the reception, we cleaned up everything and went out to eat for breakfast.

These were the days of my engagement and wedding.

Chapter 16

THE HONEYMOON

When we went back to my home, I took my wedding dress off and got my luggage to leave for the honeymoon. Walking out of my one and only home for the last time was hard on me, and I started crying. It was my security blanket, and I knew things would never be the same once I walked out that door.

The best man and his wife drove us to the airport, and then we got onto the plane. I now remember that I didn't sleep at all the night before the wedding and didn't sleep at all the wedding night. The last I slept was the night before our rehearsal day (the day before the wedding). I was too excited to sleep on the plane.

We flew to San Juan, Puerto Rico to get on our ship, the Royal Caribbean called *Song of the Sea* or *Song of Norway,* something like that. We took a seven-day, seven-night Caribbean cruise. We went to six different islands: San Juan, Barbados, St. Thomas, Antigua, St. Martinique, and St. Martin. We got on our ship and found our cabin. The ship was huge and beautiful. We looked around and then it was getting time to leave the port.

We went up to the top deck to watch as we left. The sun was starting to set. While we're standing there, I was leaning on the rail to watch us leave and then I literally fell asleep while standing up. I had been awake for sixty hours straight. That had been the longest I had gone without sleep to this date, even with my recent insomnia. As soon as we left, we headed back to the cabin and I went to sleep.

The next day, we learned where we were going to dine. We were assigned a certain table where we would go to all week. We were placed with three other couples around our age that were all on their honeymoons as well. One couple was from Los Angeles, and they were both cops. Another couple was from Detroit, Michigan and worked at Ford Motor Company or General Motors. I am not sure which one now. The last couple was from Quebec, and he was a fashion designer. My husband and I seemed to hit it off good with the cops from L.A.

Each evening we had the same waiter, and there was a different theme each night for our meal. They would celebrate a different country each night. They would wear the outfits from that country, prepare authentic food from that country, do some traditions from that country, and have a parade around all the tables for that country. One night, they wore a dragon and went around our tables. When it was "America night," we had an alcohol shot that was striped red, white, and blue. They would do tricks with toothpicks, napkins, food, and fire. They would make things out of them too. The buffets were amazing with ice sculptures and butter sculptures, all kinds of food sculptures, and an assortment of food. They had three different times you could eat each meal, including breakfast, lunch, and dinner, and even the midnight buffets.

We went to shows. We didn't gamble much. We toured all the islands. The banana trees were neat. The water was crystal clear, then it was a pretty green, and a pretty blue the farther you got out. The sand was white, and you could see the bottom through the water since it was so clean and clear.

When we rode in cars, the drivers drove on the opposite side of the road and drove really fast, never using their breaks. They used their horns to get people and animals out of their way, which scared the crap out of me. The people who lived there were poor. They lived in little shacks with dirt floors, and chickens and goats ran around in the yard.

We went on a submarine tour, under the water, and saw sharks, and even a shipwreck. I took pictures out of the portholes. I was a little claustrophobic with that, but they had cold air vents blowing on us so that helped. When we went snorkeling, I couldn't figure out how to only breathe through my mouth with the tube and the mask over my eyes and nose. I started to panic, so I took the tube out of my mouth and just went under water, holding my breath and seeing the fish with my mask on. I kept coming up for air, but it worked out all right.

Before we ever even knew where we were going for our honeymoon, I had a dream we were in this body of water and it was very scary and eerie. I didn't know why and I didn't know where we were. Well, the one day we went on this Jolly Roger Pirate Ship. It takes you out where you can't touch and you can walk the plank and jump into the water and swim, but that day we couldn't because there were jellyfish everywhere. They were serving rum punch, and my husband got *really* drunk. He kept leaning over the side, and I was so afraid he was going to fall into the water with the jellyfish.

All of a sudden, I looked up and I looked out and there was my dream. This body of water was exactly like my dream. I started to get scared. Then the tour guide proceeded to tell us that just the day before, a man got drunk and fell overboard and drowned in this exact spot. Then I started freaking out even more. I just wanted to get off that boat and get back on the ship.

Some other guys got really drunk and started fighting, and my husband, who was already drunk, saw the fight and wanted to step in and get involved and start fighting with them too. I was doing everything I could to keep him from getting involved and just getting us back to the ship. Once on the ship, he bounced from wall to wall down the hallway to our cabin. He was so drunk. I was so relieved to get him in the cabin. I was scared, so mad at him, and embarrassed and worried and felt so alone.

One evening we were in a storm, and the waves were really bad. At dinner, the ship was rocking so bad that the water in our glasses was sideways. People wouldn't even stay for dinner. We all went back to our cabins. There were barf bags out everywhere for everyone. We could barely get up the steps. We had to hang on for dear life. We didn't get sick, but didn't feel the greatest. After being on the ship for a while and rocking with the waves, your equilibrium would get messed up and you would get off the ship on dry land and you would still be rocking. It was a weird sensation. I understood the meaning of having sea legs.

They would play island music with homemade steel drums. It was really neat. In the towns on the islands, they would beg for money. We ended up buying alcohol and bringing it home.

We made it home safely after the honeymoon. After being home even for a week, I would still feel like I was rocking with the boat. It was a weird feeling.

That was the honeymoon.

Chapter 17

WELCOME HOME

My husband carried me over the threshold. We walked in the front door to the living room, and there was a huge "Welcome Home" sign on the wall. I started to look around and I found all of my home interior pictures I had bought through the years that I was going to put up on the walls were all already hung, all our dishes were put away in the cupboards, and my husband's clothes were put away. Even all his underwear were stacked and folded perfectly in the dresser in our bedroom. He had bought a king-sized waterbed for me as my wedding present, and I bought him a gun cabinet for his wedding present. All the furniture was arranged, everything was done.

My mother-in-law and my husband's aunt went into the house when we were on the honeymoon and did it all. Now I guess this was supposed to be a surprise for us and a nice gesture on behalf of my mother-in-law to help us out and even though I tried to be happy about it, I was very, very upset about it. I wanted the joy of hanging my pictures and putting them where I wanted them. Once again, now I didn't feel like this was my home at all. It is my husband and his mother's home.

For six months, when I would go visit my mom and dad, I would cry every time I left. I didn't want to go back to the house where I now lived. We had a party at our house and invited family and friends to watch us open all of our wedding presents. His parents got us a washer and dryer. My parents got us a set of goldware.

After we got settled in and went back to work, I told my true feelings about what my mother-in-law did with the house with my co-workers. None of them could believe it and were upset too and said I had every reason to feel the way I was feeling. My mother-in-law was determined to control us. She would keep calling me at work and upsetting me and I told my boss, and my boss was getting upset with her and would answer the phone and tell her I was busy. I continued working for a while longer and then we all received bad news that our company had been bought out and we were all losing our jobs. Slowly, one by one, we would get called into the office and someone else was let go. They ended up shutting the whole factory down and only one went on to the other plant that bought us out. Everyone else had to find new jobs.

There were quite a few married couples that both worked there, and it was devastating to their households. They both needed to find work now. I found work at a factory in the town I lived in. It was an office job doing data entry on the computer. They sewed seats for RVs. They didn't work on Sundays. My boss gave me a key because I needed to go in on Sunday evenings and print off updates and distribute them so everyone had them first thing Monday morning. It was so scary going in there by myself. No one was there and all the lights were off in the factory. I would have my brother go with me so I wouldn't be alone.

It reminded me when I was a kid and they held a haunted factory there for Halloween one year and I went. There were these windows that divided the office from the factory. Behind one window, someone was dressed up scary and would bang on the window and scare you. Then you came to a second window waiting for someone to bang on that one but there was no glass in it and they came out of the window, chasing you, scaring the crap out of you.

On lunch hours, I got to answer the phone. I really liked that. I worked there for a little while, and we got bad news again. The plant was being bought back by the original owner. So guess what? We all lose our jobs again. My boss and a couple people go to the other plant to work.

My husband and I had our first fight about getting the thank-you letters done for our wedding presents. My matron of honor has now became best friends with my mother-in-law and my husband's cousin got married and moved next door. His wife becomes jealous of me and started spying on me and criticizing everything I did and her husband and my husband would drink alcohol all the time together.

We ended up putting a new roof on the house, adding a half bath in the laundry room. We took the screened in back porch and made it a living quarters and built on an outdoor deck. We ripped out bushes and re-landscaped. We put railroad ties along the driveway and planted new bushes and flowers and laid stone. We built a shed next to the house and replanted all the grass. We ended up buying more land behind our house. It was all field, so we had to plant grass. It was a really muddy mess until the grass finally came in. I found an old ceramic, very tiny doll in the dirt in the backyard without arms and legs. I cleaned it up and took it to an antique store and they put arms and legs on it for me and it became worth fifty dollars.

I had a shadow box hanging in my kitchen. It was an old sewing machine drawer that had little square holes that held different spools of thread. I put little miniature things in it. I put the doll in it. My dad came over one time and put a penny in my box too. Just like when he put the penny in my shoe at my wedding. I loved that and treasured that. My mom and dad would come over to visit, and I would give my dad grape pop. He loved it. Since he was a carpenter, he would come over to see all the things we were doing with the house. He was interested in seeing it.

***

Puppy Love

My husband, soon after we were married, bought me a puppy. His best friend's dog was pregnant by a little white poodle. Their dog was a golden cocker spaniel named Ginger. So I got one of the puppies. It was a curly white-and-gold-haired cockapoo. She had the cocker face and ears and the poodle hair. She didn't shed at all. She was about eighteen pounds when she was fully grown. She was scared to death of thunder. When it stormed, she would want to be in the vehicles, but if she couldn't be, she would scratch at the carpet, trying to dig a hole to bury herself into to get away from the storm.

When we got her fixed, she was so upset she took all of her toys and put them on a pile on the couch and laid on them and wouldn't let anyone near them. She wanted to be a mommy so bad and was so upset that she wouldn't be able to now. We took that from her, and she wasn't going to let us take her toys away from her too.

We named her Heidi. She was my baby, and I spoiled her rotten. She loved hamburgers from McDonalds and chocolate. On her birthday she got the hostess cupcakes, a hamburger, treats, a bone, and toys. She also got toys, treats, and bones for Christmas and had her own stocking and a Christmas ornament every year.

Her favorite toy was a squeaky alligator, and she loved her blue ball. She loved to play catch. You could throw it, and she would go after it. She would be on it in no time, bring it back, and want to do it some more. She would go bye-bye with me all the time. She loved to sit on my shoulders. I would give her baths and brush her teeth and buy clothes for her. I bought her sweaters and a leather coat and Halloween costumes. She was a clown and a ballerina. She would get her hair cut every couple of months, and they would put ribbons in her hair and ears. I kept up with her shots every year at the vet.

She also loved to go to my mom and dad's and run around and loved the pond. When we went to my in-laws, she would run and jump on her bed and that made her mad. She started to hate Heidi and the way I babied her (even though she had a little black poodle named Coco and she babied him). I gave Heidi her own dish of food when I fixed meals of whatever it was I fixed before we ate. She never begged for food. She potty trained pretty quickly and did very well with this. She had to be put on a chain at first for a while and then she learned to stay in her own yard. When the yard was all tore up from replanting grass, she only had mud to go potty in. It was a pain always wiping her paws down with water and drying them off before she could come into the house, but I did it anyway.

She would go to the fireworks with us. She loved the people, sights, and sounds. At the finale, when everyone clapped, yelled, and whistled, Heidi would howl along.

It was definitely puppy love for me.

Chapter 18

MARRIED LIFE: NOT AT ALL WHAT I EXPECTED

After the second factory I worked at closed their doors, I decided to stay at home and take up babysitting. My mother-in-law and my husband made it very, very clear to me that if he works and I stay home, I must keep the house completely spotless and have meals prepared and laundry done at all times and that there is no exception to the rules. The home was kept like a *Better Homes & Garden* magazine ad. The windows were washed inside and out as well as both sides of the screens. We didn't have a dishwasher, so dishes had to be washed, rinsed, dried, and put away. Laundry was washed, dried, folded and put away. I dusted and swept all the time, and everything was picked up and put in its proper place at all times. I had eyes continually watching my every move I made.

My mother-in-law (who would do surprise visits), my husband, my matron of honor (who also stopped buy on surprise visits and report back to my mother-in-law) were the main watchers. Besides that, my neighbor who was the jealous cousin was now friends with my mother-in-law as well. I could never relax in my own home or feel comfortable or at ease. I felt like I was walking on eggshells the whole time.

I ended up babysitting seven different families and thirteen different kids for quite a few years. I also worked for Avon and held a lot of those home parties where you buy stuff. I did Tupperware,

Pampered Chef, Home Interiors, candle parties, lingerie, baskets, and other home decoration parties. Parties, parties, and more parties. I handled all the finances. I also wrote some poems in my spare time. One poem was turned into a song with sheet music.

My husband would work second shift, so I made big lunches instead of suppers. He wouldn't get home until after eleven o'clock at night. He worked a lot of overtime, twelve-hour days and six days a week. He only took Saturdays off. He worked Sunday for the double time. Overtime was time and a half, and holidays were triple time. On Saturdays, he spent it hunting or drinking with his buddies. I would never see him. He had this attitude about him that he was invincible and had no fear of anything or anyone and could do anything he wanted.

At work, he went against the rules and didn't wear earplugs. One time hot sparks from welding went down his eardrum and burned it. We had to go to the hospital, and he had to have ear surgery. He also went bungee jumping and made me nervous the whole time. No one would climb the water tower at work to change the light bulb, so he did it. Once again, I was a nervous wreck.

Later on, he went on a hunting trip out west in the Rocky Mountains with a group of people and his uncle. I get word that a gun went off and someone was hurt badly and my husband and uncle were missing. I was a complete and utter wreck again. His uncle shot a signal shot up to let the tour guides know to come get them because they were ready to head down out of the mountains. It was snowy up there, and his gun got packed with snow, so when he shot it off, part of the barrel exploded and went right through his eye. My husband took his hat off, packed it with snow, and put it on his uncle's head and eye. He got him on a horse and rode down until they got to the guide, but then they had to go further down to the camp site, and then even further down to meet an ambulance. He was taken to a hospital and had surgery done. He lost his eye out of it. To this day, he has a glass eye. My husband was okay, but I was a wreck.

One weekend, my husband went out drinking with his buddies and relatives. Usually, they would all meet at our home, or the cousin's home next door, but this particular night they went to another house in town. I was home alone. It got to be so late that I had fallen asleep on the couch. Something startled me and I awoke. I looked around and didn't see any evidence that my husband was home yet. I got up and went to the bedroom to see if he was there. He was not. I looked in the drive and his truck was not there. I felt this panic come over me that something was very wrong.

I called the house where he was supposed to be, and they said they had no idea where he was. This was his other cousin's house. They said he left with someone else a long time ago. I went next door and woke them up. They were mad at me for waking them up in the middle of the night and they said they didn't know where he was. I called his parents. They were mad at me and said, "You know your husband is going to be mad at you for checking up on him." Time kept ticking and no word came.

As I sat and worried, night became day. It was now Sunday morning. His parents called and asked if he was back home, and I said no. We then decided to do a search for him. They started driving around to see if he might be in a ditch somewhere. We called the emergency rooms with no sign of him. We called the two cousins again, but they didn't have any information and didn't show any type of concern at all. By this point, the parents who thought I was crazy for worrying started to worry.

We called the cousins yet again, and my mother-in-law was there expressing great concern and if they knew anything, they better start talking. The cousin's wife decided to start talking to her husband, and he filled her in on what was going on. She told him to tell us as well. Apparently, they got bored at their little party and decided to go into the next state to a bar. My husband was drinking and drove his truck there, while the other guys drove some of their vehicles too. Right at four o'clock in the morning, when I woke up startled the night before, my husband was pulled over by the police, charged with a DUI and thrown in jail, while his truck was impounded. That terrible feeling I had at that moment was for a good reason!

His cousin was with him when it happened and knew all about it and ended up getting a ride home with the other guys. He then went to bed, not bothering to tell anyone what had happened. None of the guys bothered to speak up, and even after being asked several times, they still lied until they finally came clean. My husband didn't call because he was passed out in the cell, or he tried but couldn't get through because I was on the phone looking for him and he was only allowed one phone call. His driving was always reckless, whether he was drinking or not, and I was always nervous riding with him no matter what it was he was driving, like his truck, four-wheeler, or Jet Ski.

Now his mother and I were relieved he was alive, but now we were furious! This was before ATM machines at the bank, and the bank was closed on Sunday of course. We needed cash to bail him out of jail because they only took cash. Fortunately, I stashed cash in a hiding place in the house. Since I controlled the finances and my husband liked to spend all the money on hunting, booze, and gambling, I started hiding money so he wouldn't spend it all. Well, I had enough cash saved up to bail him out of jail.

His mother drove and I rode with her to pick him up. When we got there, he was so drunk he reeked of alcohol. His mother made him get in the backseat while I sat up front and she drove. She yelled at him the whole way home. I was quiet the whole way until I asked where he was. He didn't want to answer me, and his mother said, "Your wife just asked you a question and you had better answer her."

We didn't end up getting his truck back until later that week. He lost his license, paid a big fine, and did community service. He could only drive to work and back. It costs us money to get his truck back too, besides the money for bail I had already paid.

After we got home, I drove by myself over to the cousin's house and laid into his cousin for not coming clean with me and for causing me and the family to worry for hours. His wife let me yell at him all I wanted since she agreed with me. I was so mad at everyone involved. They all knew and didn't care that I was worried and wouldn't tell me where he was.

On another weekend, we rode our four-wheeler to a nearby lake with another couple we were friends with who lived in the same town as us. They had a four-wheeler as well, so we rode to the lake together. There was this party, and once again, my husband had to drink. We went to leave the party with the other couple on our four-wheelers, and my husband decided to drive after drinking. Apparently, he hadn't learned from his previous episode. Four-wheelers were not really supposed to be driven on the roads either. They were backcountry roads with loose gravel on them. This can make them almost like ice when you have to stop fast, making you slide and making it very easy to lose control.

We started to head home when a cop came up behind us. The other couple stopped, but not my husband. He floored it to get away from the cops. I kept begging him to stop, but he wouldn't listen to me at all. You can never argue with a drunk. I started shaking because I was afraid. I was afraid of getting into trouble and going to jail but I was also afraid we were going to wreck. I became a complete and utter nervous wreck. He continued to fly through all of the stop signs, not stopping for anything. I was so afraid I was going to die.

There I was, raised in a good Christian home, and going to jail was never supposed to happen to me or anyone in my family. My husband had already been there once and didn't want to go again, so he outran the cop, but that made me afraid that I was going to end up in jail if we did get caught. What was my family going to think? I could only imagine what they thought about my husband now. And if I didn't end up there, what if I ended up dead? He always seemed to put me between a rock and a hard place. I was never able to escape the situations he would put me in.

He continued to drive until we reached the other couples' home. Once we got there, he finally stopped. I jumped off right away and ran to the other side of their home to get away from my husband. I was so upset with him. My nerves were so bad that I had to go to the bathroom. They were not back yet. My husband wouldn't let me go home to use the bathroom. He wanted to stay there until they came home. I was so desperate that I pulled my pants down on the side of their house and had diarrhea on their lawn. My whole body was shaking. My stomach hurt so badly.

The couple finally showed up and the cops let them off, but the cops were not happy with what my husband did. Luckily nothing came about it and he got off that time without any repercussions. I then got put down by my husband because I couldn't hold it, and he showed no compassion, kindness, or sympathy whatsoever of what he just made me go through. He always made it seem like it was all my own problem or my own fault. He never showed me any respect or understanding.

On yet another occasion, after my husband had been drinking, he wanted to drive around and go groundhog hunting and wanted me to go with him. I did not think any of this was a good idea, but I couldn't argue with a drunk. We got into his truck. He was driving. We were on the back roads when he saw a groundhog. He decided he was going to try and shoot it while driving, being drunk, and use the gun over my lap through the passenger side window.

Once again, I was afraid for our lives. I was afraid we were going to wreck or that I would get shot. I tried to get him to stop and that made him mad. He swung his arm, smacking me in the face, causing my glasses to go flying. Once again, I was put in a position that I was fearing for my life and my options were to not say anything and continue to fear until something terrible happened, or to try to stop it but get hit by him.

He had successfully put me back into that spot of being between a rock and a hard place with no way out. His mind games were destroying me. I was getting so tired of these mental games he would play. The mental, emotional, and now physical abuse was becoming a real problem. His drinking was a huge problem. He was turning into a very mean drunk.

When we get back, I get a hold of his parents and they came over. His dad has a talk with him in the garage, and his mother had a talk with me in the house. She lectured me that I needed to keep my mouth shut. See, they handle disagreements by giving the silent treatment to each other and won't speak to each other for days or weeks at a time, which causes them to hold grudges forever. If you try to communicate in a healthy manner, that is "picking a fight," and so it was my fault that he hit me. I needed to learn to shut my mouth. It didn't matter if I was scared for my life or not.

When we got out to the garage, my husband had tears in his eyes and he was sorry. His parents lectured that we needed to get things straightened out before we have any children. I believed him. Looking back, it was just another mind game. He brought the tears on just for his parents to see and to try and confuse me. As time went on, he was concerned to have children because he didn't want the housework to slide in any way, shape, or form. He kept threatening me about that over and over again.

This was not at all what I expected married life to be.

Chapter 19

BABY NUMBER 1

One day, I did laundry. I loved hanging it on the line because it would smell so good when it was dry. While outside hanging the clothes up, I had a very sharp pain in my side. I finish hanging them up and had another. By the time I got inside, it hit again and this time it didn't let up. The pain was so bad it made me go to my knees. I thought my insides were exploding. I crawled to the bathroom to try and get some Tylenol. It just kept getting worse. By this point, I was in tears. I crawled to the phone in the kitchen and called my dad to come over. My husband was at work. My dad came over and took me to the hospital. I was in pain the whole time.

When I got to the hospital, I couldn't sit still. I ended up in the bathroom, throwing up. They ran tests and admitted me. I was passing a kidney stone. The pain was so bad. I would try to squeeze my side, pace up and down, and move side to side, anything to make the pain stop. It took my breath away. Then came the IV. My veins are small and hidden, so the nurses always have a hard time getting the IV to go in without blowing the vein. It was such a relief when the IV went in and stayed in. When they shot morphine in, I had sweet relief. I instantly felt the effects, and it felt so good not to have the pain.

My dad felt bad for me. He knew how it felt since he had one. I ended up there for a week. My doctor had one and knew how it felt, so he ordered that I could get as much morphine as I wanted. Another man I knew was in there for the same reason, so we could sympathize with each other. We would talk. He was from the same town. We joked and said it must be in the water. I finally passed it.

On another occasion, I needed all of my wisdom teeth taken out. They had to pull two and surgically remove the other two. My dad took me again for this procedure. They did all of them at one time. They put me out. When I was coming to, I was not happy. I was in a panic. I threw all the gauze that was in my mouth across the room and was swinging my arms. My dad was trying to calm me down. I did not like my mouth stuffed and was very claustrophobic. I had been buried in the sand as a kid up to my face and could tolerate it but not a huge fan. For whatever reason, I did not like this. My mouth finally healed up, and I was okay. As time continued, my claustrophobia became much worse.

By this point, I was two years into our marriage and it was August 19, 1991 (our second anniversary). We got invited to go on a four-wheeler trip up north with two other couples, the one couple being our best man and matron of honor. We all slept in the same tent together. Our best man and matron of honor and the other couple were extremely tight with each other, and they would make it quite obvious to everyone. I would feel uncomfortable and felt that I was just a third wheel and didn't belong there. This happened every time we would go out with these two couples.

My matron of honor would glare at me and ignore me at times when we would go out. When I would confront her about it, she would act like she didn't know what I was talking about and that it was all in my head and that I had a problem. Looking back, these were mind games. I was being taught not to trust my gut feelings and that everything was my problem.

On one of the days we were there, the guys went riding up the hills and the girls stayed back at the tent. Later, the two guys came back and said that my husband had wrecked and flew off the four-wheeler. Part of me was glad I was not with him and the other part was worried about him. He finally got back to the tent with his four-wheeler. He ended up being okay. I didn't want to ride with him. I wanted to have a nice, fun, relaxing time. I didn't want to be stressed out. I begged him to please take it easy and be careful, especially when I was riding with him. All three of us couples split up to have alone time. Well, we parked the four-wheeler on a private trail and made love on the four-wheeler outside in the wilderness. The rest of the trip went well, and we all got back home safely.

A month later, I was at the county fair. I enjoyed the fair food and going to the demo derby. My husband didn't go because he was working. I always had to go by myself anywhere. After the derby, I got in my car and I didn't feel good at all. I thought I was going to throw up and I thought it was from the fair food. I drove home with the windows down. I didn't end up getting sick. I tried to take it easy.

Around the same week, my great aunt and uncle's house and belongings were put up at auction. I decided to go. I bid on this quilt because I thought it was the one that had parts of my grandmother's wedding dress in it. I ended up getting it. The neighbor by my parent's house helped make the quilt at our church with my great aunt. It meant a lot to her, and she wanted to know if she could have it. She said she had my grandmother's wooden rocking chair. My grandmother always kept it in the kitchen next to the wood burner. She said I could have that in exchange. I didn't want to give up the quilt at first but decided to make the exchange.

As the week went on, I was still not feeling well and it was time for my monthly. I was always on time, like clockwork, but not this time. I started to wonder what was going on. Then it dawned on me. I could be pregnant! I decided to get a home pregnancy test. I got home and read the instructions, nervous as all get out. I did what it said and then I waited. I was so nervous. As I went to look at it, sure enough there was a plus sign, clear as day.

Oh my gosh, I'm pregnant! This was so ironic because the neighbor I just did the exchange with was joking and said I needed the rocking chair to rock my baby. I put the rocking chair in the kitchen like my grandma had done. I also found it ironic that I made out with my first boyfriend at the fair, started my womanhood at the fair, and then got my first sickness of my first pregnancy at the fair too. There must have been something about that fair, I swear. We had a long history together.

I later discovered that the reason I was sick at the fair was from the gas fumes from the demo derby. Every time I smelled gas, I would throw up. I couldn't pump my own gas. The smell never bothered me before, but my body didn't like it at all while being pregnant. I went out and bought a baby calendar to follow along with the growth of my baby in my belly. I threw up the first sixty days in a row. Once it was after I ate breakfast at McDonalds. I got sick in their bathroom. I had saltine crackers by my bed in the mornings. I ended up losing ten pounds from getting sick.

As a little time went on, the couple we were on the four-wheeler trip with announced she was pregnant too. We discovered our due dates were very close too, May 21, 1992. This was her second, and she had a C-section for her first, so she would have to have a C-section again this time too. As we calculated back for the time of conception, it was on the four-wheeler trip on my husband and mine second anniversary while we made love on the four-wheeler. Obviously, we weren't the only ones with that idea that day too.

We were by a lake up there. The name of the lake was Avery Lake. A TV show on at the time was *Murphy Brown,* and she had a baby on the show she named Avery. The couple who were also pregnant were going to name their baby Avery because that was where they conceived, but they changed their minds and came up with a different name.

During my pregnancy, I went on a bus tour to a town that had the largest basket in the world. There was even a building that looked like a basket. The diesel fuel fumes were too much for me, and I got sick in the bathroom on the bus. I had went with other ladies. Other than that, the trip went pretty well. I noticed I started craving tuna fish sandwiches and ruby red grapefruit juice and I had to have them together. I ate and drank so much of this during my pregnancy that my first-born can't stand either to this day. I ate so much that she is filled for life.

As the other lady's and my stomachs grew, my husband made a comment one day when we were in the front yard that we looked like cattle grazing in a field. The other lady shot him daggers with her eyes. Such a kind-hearted man, that husband of mine. It led me to wanting to stay pregnant forever. As long as my baby was in my belly, it would be safe from all harm and with me wherever I went. It would always be protected. I was so afraid for my baby to face this world. I would read books out loud while pregnant so the baby would recognize my voice.

May 20, 1992 arrived. It was ten thirty in the evening, and my husband was playing Nintendo. I was on the couch. I felt a pain and thought I had to go to the bathroom. I stood up, and for some reason I didn't think I could make it, so I went to the kitchen instead. As soon as I hit the kitchen, my water broke. Not just a little, but a massive flow of water. I yelled at my husband that my water broke.

He didn't want to stop playing his video game and said, "Are you sure you aren't peeing? You said you had to pee."

I said, "I'm not peeing. My water broke! I need some clothes and towels please. Hurry up! Heidi, our dog, is going to get into it." He stopped his game, unhappily, and got me towels and clothes. We cleaned up, and I put a towel between my legs and went to the hospital. Once I was at the hospital, I started having contractions. They made me sign in at the front desk first, and I was leaving puddles of water everywhere. The towel I had between my legs was completely drenched now.

The lady that we went on the trip with was already in the hospital. She had her C-section done earlier that day. It was a girl. It was on May 20, 1992.

As they wheeled me upstairs and got me into a bed, I found myself laying in the hallway. Everybody and their brother decided to have their babies this night, so all of the rooms were full. Mothers were lining up in the hallways, me being one of them. I could hear other moms screaming in pain. It wasn't a pleasant thing to hear. I was getting a little scared, nervous, and anxious. This was my first time. I didn't know what to expect, and they were so busy. I thought they were going to forget about me and just leave me in the hallway to fend for myself.

The hospital had a three-room setup. You went to the labor room, then the delivery room, then to your room after delivery. Well, I never made it to the labor room. When they got me to the delivery room, I couldn't believe it. I saw my nurse, and it happened to be my ex-boyfriend's wife. The couple who spread terrible rumors about me in high school. Oh boy! This is great! I sure hoped she had matured since high school and treats me well. I was anxious about that now too. Just my luck! Well, needless to say, she treated me very well. Actual bonding occurred, forgiveness happened, and we were friends after it all. Anyways, back to my delivery. It didn't take me long to get to ten centimeters. However, trying to get the baby out was another story. I pushed and pushed and continued to push.

See, two weeks earlier, I had went to the doctor because I noticed I wasn't urinating very well. The doctor disregarded it. His bedside manner was very poor. I was going to him because the other lady we hung out with had him too. She agreed he didn't have a good bedside manner but she loved him. Me on the other hand, not so much. I had been so thirsty and drank all the time but not emptying like I should. Since the doctor disregarded it, I trusted his judgment and thought it was normal. How was I to know? This was my first time with this.

Well, I pushed and pushed until the baby came out. It was just the nurse and I the whole time. The doctor was so busy that he would just peek in and leave to another room the whole time. He finally came in and stayed when the baby was coming out. I delivered a 7 lbs. 8.5 oz. baby girl. She was 20.5 inches long. She arrived that Thursday at 12:34 a.m., just after midnight on her due date. My delivery was just like my mom's. It was very fast. My water broke at home at 10:30 p.m., and my baby girl arrived just two hours later. We named her after the great grandmother's names on both sides of the family. Her dad's mother's mother and her mom's mother's mother.

She was born May 21, 1992. I was born on the twenty-first as well at 12:30 am. She was put in my arms. She had a cone head from trying to come out. She didn't have any hair. She had a pink birthmark on her forehead, an angel kiss. She also had a pink birthmark on the back of her neck, a stork bite. She has the same marks as me!

She had blue eyes, and still has them to this day, which was strange since her dad and I both have brown eyes, and brown eyes are supposed to be dominant. She had all ten fingers and toes and was very healthy. I wanted to hold her longer but I just couldn't. I started having sever pain in my stomach. They took her to the nursery.

I still had to deliver the afterbirth. The nurse would push on my tummy. I started hemorrhaging. Fistfuls of clots kept coming out and wouldn't stop. The nurse became very concerned and called the doctor back in. He came in right away, and they put a catheter in me and started draining the urine from my bladder.

When my baby's head moved down in my belly, it was pushing on my bladder, making my bladder literally fall asleep like when you lay on your arm or sit on your leg and it cuts off the circulation. That is why I couldn't pee. They ended up draining gallons and gallons of urine. The bleeding finally subsided. I had lost so much blood. My bladder had expanded so much to hold all that urine. The baby didn't have much room to come out. That is why I had such a rough time pushing her out. They said I was lucky my bladder didn't burst because that would have killed both of us.

I did end up having a lot of problems with my bladder after that though. I had interstitial cystitis. I could no longer drink tea, coffee, or pop with dark colors, or any drink with caffeine. It would feel like a bladder infection, but it would spasm and antibiotics would not help.

Once I was taken to my room, I was so weak from losing so much blood and I went into shock. My whole body was shaking uncontrollably. I tried to tell the nurses something was wrong, and they came in and saw me but just walked out and disregarded it. They were too busy to pay attention to me. After quite a while, being scared and praying that I wouldn't die, the shaking finally subsided and I went to sleep. I kept waking up and looked around and would be scared.

My husband did bring me a dozen red roses and did the dishes, laundry, and ran the sweeper. I finally got discharged but found myself still struggling even six months after my delivery. The other mom would be glad when her baby would go to sleep because she was tired and wanted a break. With me, I was beyond tired. I was exhausted and couldn't enjoy a break. I felt like passing out. When I got home, I had a white wicker bassinet that I was borrowing from my husband's side of the family. We had done the nursery with little sheep in mint green. Her crib had a white canopy on top.

When we got home, Heidi, our dog, was so curious. She would get on the couch and keep looking into the bassinet. She wanted to be a mommy so badly, and her mother instincts kicked into overdrive. She became a real mother hen.

One day when my baby was taking a nap and I was in the backyard hanging clothes, I had the baby monitor outside on the deck with me, and Heidi was outside with me. The next-door neighbor saw me and asked me to come over to check out her recipe. Her garage door was open, and it led to her kitchen. While I was over there, my baby started crying over the monitor. I had left it there on the deck since I was only going to be gone for a minute.

Well, Heidi was still outside and heard her over the monitor and ran into the neighbor's garage to the kitchen door and barked, and barked, and barked. I went out to see what she was barking at, and she was running back and forth from me to the monitor, trying to get me to walk toward the house. As I did, I heard my baby crying. Heidi was the best mother hen ever. Whenever I let my girl out in the backyard to play, Heidi had to be right by her side the whole time. She watched over her continuously.

As my baby got older and learned how to crawl, I had to put Heidi's food up. She would crawl over to it, grab a handful of dry dog food, and shove it into her mouth. I would have to pry her fingers open to get the dog food out of her hands and finger sweep her mouth to get all of the dog food out.

My mother instincts kicked into overdrive as well. My senses heightened. My smell and hearing became very strong. I became a light sleeper and could hear everything.

When my milk came in, I was in so much pain. I thought my breasts were going to explode. They hurt so badly. I even got a fever of 104 degrees. I remember lying in the bathtub, trying to let them drain for some relief. I did breastfeed for a while. There was so much pressure that it would squirt into my baby's throat and she would start to choke. It took us a while to get the hang of it. I could squirt clear across the room with as much pressure that I had. I remember wearing the pads and being soaked and sticky. Also, going to the bathroom was no fun either since I had to wait for the stitches to heal and the bleeding to stop.

I remember when I gave my baby her first bath. It was in the kitchen at the kitchen sink. I put a towel down and laid her on the counter. I filled the sink with warm water and used a little washcloth with Baby Magic wash. I would hold her like a football with her head just over the sink to wash her head, being sure not to get any water in her eyes or ears. This part really scared me at first, but I got the hang of it in no time. I wiped her face, neck, ears, and little body. I put alcohol on a Q-tip and rubbed it around the umbilical cord and would continue to wash her arms, legs, hands, and feet. I would rinse her and then dry her, put lotion on her, and then add a diaper and sleeper. She would smell so good. I love that baby smell. I had a plastic yellow duck that had a thermometer on it that floated in the water to get the right temp for the water.

We eventually graduated to a blue plastic bath she laid in and then a ring to sit in inside the bathtub. She had lots of bath toys, and that was when we sang a lot of Christian kid songs. I lost all my baby weight pretty fast. Breastfeeding helped with that.

I would have her sleep in the bassinet right next to my side of the bed. I would lay her on her side and keep blankets away from her face. I was so afraid of the sudden infant death syndrome where the child can die in their sleep. I always kept a close eye on her. Eventually she moved into her crib in her room with the monitor. I was always scared for her to be around water as well. I didn't want her to drown.

We read a lot of books, including Bible stories. She learned her colors, numbers, letters, shapes, time, and eventually money. We read a lot of Dr. Seuss books over and over and over again. We had to watch Barney and all of the Disney movies. She hated wearing shoes and socks, and even clothes for that matter. She learned how to tie her shoes as she got older. At home she was happy with a diaper and a onesie. I got her clothes at Peaches for Little People, Carter's, and Osh Kosh. I had went other places as well. We went to Sam's Club to stock up on diapers, wipes, and formula.

We went through the stages of bottle feeding and burping. I always had a cloth diaper around for a burp rag. I was always ready for her to spit up or throw up. When she had a bellyache, I took warm water in a bottle and dropped in a few powdered party mints and let them dissolve and shook it up. Instant mint water. I had her drink it so she could burp easier, and it settled her belly. She never sucked her thumb and didn't really care for the pacifier much either. We soon got to the baby food and Sippy cups. We loved the Hawaiian Delight and Juicy Juice. We took her Cheerios and a Sippy cup in a diaper bag with us to church to help keep her quiet and entertained. I kept a baby book going as well as pictures as she grew.

She loved to play with her Barbies and her dollhouse. She had a Little Tikes kitchen set that was set up in the kitchen. The kitchen was really big with a long wall, so my baby's kitchen went up along that wall well. She loved to play with it while I worked in the kitchen. She had a ladybug car and a little tikes washer and dryer with an iron and iron board as well. I still wish we had them. We ended up donating them to our church for the preschool that they held.

As she got older, her hair finally grew and popped out with such awesome curly hair. She was tall for her age too. She got that from her dad and his side of the family. We would listen to country music and dance together in the kitchen. She liked her swing, walker, and Johnnie Jumper. I hung it from a doorway, and she would bounce, bounce, and bounce. She loved it. We had a stroller to go on walks with. She got a wagon and a red tricycle too. We ended up getting her a swing set and jungle gym all wooden in the backyard. It took a while to build. It had a slide, rope, pole, monkey bars, sandbox, bridge, several decks to climb with a roof, and swings. It was awesome and any kids' dream.

When she got older, she started helping me in the kitchen right away and loved to help mommy cook and bake. She also became a fan of the American Girl Doll collection. She loved cake. It was so hard for me to keep her out of her birthday cakes before the parties. She put her fingers into her Winnie the Pooh cake one year, and it took me a while to piece it back together and have it presentable for the party.

As she grew, she learned quickly and was very smart. However, learning to go potty was a whole other story. I had a little wooden potty chair for her. I really struggled with her to figure out what would work for her to go. We did the reward board, and after so many sticker stars, she would get a reward. That didn't work. We tried pretty panties or ones with princesses on them and said that the princesses couldn't get dirty. That didn't work. I bought her a doll with her own little potty chair and a book that went with it. That didn't work either. It seemed like I was trying everything and nothing would work. Then I found some potty videos for kids. She loved watching those videos, and finally, that is what convinced her to finally give in and become potty trained. She thought there were snakes in the toilet that would get her.

My mother-in-law came over the first week we were home a lot. She fixed meals, did dishes, and helped look after her new grand-daughter for me while I tried to get better and adjusted to everything. I was so grateful for the help but scared at the same time. I was being watched and judged for every little move I made or didn't make. I was on edge and just couldn't relax even in my own house.

This led to my neighbors next door, the cousins of my husband's. They were a niece and nephew to my mother-in-law. Conveniently, they could watch my every move when my mother-in-law wasn't around and would report back to her about everything I did. The neighbor was so jealous of me and would watch and judge everything she saw. She spread rumors about me to try and make me look bad.

She hated when I hung our clothes on the clothesline in the backyard, especially our underwear. We were going to hang underwear in her trees one night but we didn't. The neighbors on the other side of my house were having a party outside and saw me. I filled them in on what I was going to do and why. They thought it was hilarious. I got along with them well.

She also didn't like that I wore my bikini while mowing grass, so I decided one time, when it was really hot nonetheless, to wear this long winter coat while mowing the grass to see if I could get a charge out of her.

One time my baby girl was really fussy. I had went down the whole list of feeding, burping, changing her diaper, holding her, and dancing to country music with her in the kitchen. Nothing was working, so I put her in the walker outside in the backyard for a change of scenery and to take a quick break. She continued to cry. Heidi, our dog, laid outside next to her. I was on the deck, and sure enough, the neighbor was looking out her window. She couldn't see me, only my daughter. She went around telling everyone that I was a terrible mother because I left my daughter in the backyard by herself crying.

Another time, I had pulled into my driveway and my baby was sleeping in her car seat. I left her sleeping while I brought in the groceries. She had woke up and was crying before I got back out to the car. Once again, the neighbors saw this and spread more bad rumors about me. I always pulled my car completely into my garage after that.

Thank goodness no one would listen to the rumors and knew me well enough, and knew her well enough to know what was true and what wasn't. The fact remained though—I couldn't just relax and be me in my own backyard, driveway, or even inside my own home for that matter. I had eyes watching my every move.

We had this competition thing going on all the time with the friends from the wedding being they had their baby the same time we had ours. She was another source of eyes to go back to the mother-in-law since they were very close. I couldn't win, no matter how hard I tried.

They were going to baptize their baby and thought about getting a professional picture of her in her gown. She had told me about it and didn't do it. I thought it was a great idea, so I did it and it made her mad. I had my baby's picture in her gown taken at Kmart. They caught a good one of her sitting up, looking up, with her hands together with a light shining down on her like she was looking up at Jesus. It was beautiful.

In my opinion, they only baptized their baby for show anyways. They never went to church, so why would they want a picture anyhow?

When we decided to have our baby baptized, I took it very seriously. I wanted my husband to be baptized with her since he never had been. He agreed to it. I thought things with him would get better because of it, but instead things got so much worse. It was like Satan was pissed off for taking one of his souls and he came back with a vengeance to get it back and he succeeded. The drinking got much worse. We had a party at our house after church for the baptismal.

On a positive note, my dad adored his new granddaughter. As she got a little older, she grew to love him too and called him grandpica. They would feed the fish together in my dad's pond. They would go in the shed and take a handful of fish pellets and walk out to the pond to feed them. Heidi liked eating what was dropped. The food smelled like dog food. My dad would plant cherry tomatoes in his garden just for her and would lift her up so she could pick sweet cherries from the tree.

At Christmas, I started a tradition of buying new Christmas ornaments every year for my daughter to have when she got older. I would put the year and her name on them. The ornaments usually related to something that happened in that year. This is a tradition we still have today.

This was my baby number one, my sweet little girl.

Chapter 20

BITTERSWEET

On February 14, 1994 I became pregnant again. That summer we decided to go on a houseboat trip for the first time with several other couples. It was down in Cumberland Lake in Kentucky. We went in July. As time got closer, we went to one of the couples' houses to make plans. I noticed that she had the exact same picture hanging on her wall as my parents did. I found this really strange, and it made me think about my parents.

The group had heard of a haunted bar in Cincinnati and wanted to stop on the way down before we got on the houseboat. It was haunted by a woman who was murdered when she was pregnant. It is said if a pregnant woman goes into the bar and smells the scent of roses, it is too late. Whoever smells the roses will either lose the baby, have someone close to her die, or she will die herself. Naturally, I am the one pregnant. Everyone else wanted to do this, but not me.

As the time of the trip got closer, I did not want to go at all. I was terrified. I had a really bad feeling something really bad was going to happen. I begged my husband that we don't go, and he became very upset with me and had no understanding whatsoever. He pretty much forced me to go. My husband's parents were watching our daughter for us while we were gone. We got down there safely and didn't stop at that bar on the way down. I just prayed we wouldn't on the way back either.

When we got down there, everything was going okay, but I still had this heaviness on me that something bad was going to happen. I had made homemade cinnamon rolls for everyone, and they all loved them. I also made a macaroni chicken salad, and everyone ate and loved that too. We would have ham sandwiches with it for lunch. For suppers, we would grill different meats. There was a lot of drinking of course.

We took the Jet Ski with us as well. There was a gift shop on the dock before we got on our houseboat. We got our own room on the boat. We would explore with the boat during the day and tie the boat up to the trees on the shore at night. We used soap and shampoo in the lake to clean up. We had inner tubes we floated on. Some would jump off the side of the boat into the water, which was pretty high up. I wouldn't do it because I was about five months pregnant. I didn't feel the greatest at one point, so I laid down during the day for a while.

One of the days we went to a waterfall that was really high. It was off a cliff. It was said that others had tried to jump off it, so a bunch of the guys decided they were going to climb the cliff and jump off through the waterfalls. My husband was one of them. I didn't want him to go, but he did it anyway. There was one woman who did it as well. They all wore life jackets, thank goodness! As I watched from below, I was a nervous wreck because I was afraid that my husband was going to get hurt or die. They all jumped off the cliff.

About halfway down, the woman who jumped had bent her legs instead of keeping them straight. By the time she hit the water, she landed on her butt and lower back. The force was so bad that when she came up she couldn't move or breathe. We were so glad she had a life jacket on. After quite a while, we were finally able to get her on a Jet Ski and back onto the houseboat. She just laid on the floor and couldn't breathe or move. It had hit her spine and knocked the air right out of her. Even though we had EMTs on the boat amongst ourselves, no one had any compassion for her to get her back to shore and off to a hospital. No one wanted their trip ruined. She had just stayed on the boat with us and suffered. I felt so bad for her and couldn't believe how everyone was reacting to it.

When our trip was over and we got back to the dock, they had went straight to the hospital and it was a good thing they did. She was all messed up inside from the force when she hit and had internal bleeding. They admitted her. It took her a long time to recover, but she did.

As I got to an area where there was a phone, since we didn't have access to getting ahold of anyone while on the boat, I realized my parents had tried to reach me and I called right away. My dad was taken to the hospital and admitted. Now all I really wanted to do was get straight home. I was so worried, and my bad feelings were starting to actually happen. I knew something was wrong. You see, three years earlier, my father was diagnosed with leukemia. He had refused any treatment and was given three years to live.

On the way home, we didn't stop at that bar. I was so glad that we didn't go there. As soon as we got back, I went straight to my childhood home and picked up my mom and brother and had my daughter with me and we all went to the hospital. My dad had stayed for a month in the hospital before being moved to the nursing home. I would take my daughter, pick up my mom and brother, and would see my dad every single day that he was in the hospital, with the exception of one day. That day was my anniversary and my husband took me out, but I had a miserable time because all I could think about was my dad.

Finally, the doctor had us schedule a family meeting with him to discuss what we should all do because the hospital couldn't do anything more for him. We had to make the decision to have him come home and we would take care of him or to have him go to a nursing home. My dad wanted to go to a nursing home and the doctor agreed that with all the circumstances with me being pregnant and couldn't lift, and my mother and brother not being able to observe my dad when he needed help, the best option would be to have him placed in a home. It was the hardest decision to make, and I felt so guilty. My dad raised me all those years, and now I couldn't take care of him when he needed me.

After we moved him into the home, I continued to see him every day. I had noticed when we moved him, he was walking with that old man shuffle. He just scooted his feet across the floor without picking his legs up and walking. This was the first time I ever saw my dad as being old. He never looked or acted old until now. It was a real eye opener and was so hard to watch. My dad shared a room with a man who had constant hiccups. Dad loved to watch baseball, and they had went on strike so he couldn't watch it on TV and that didn't make him very happy. I noticed every day he kept getting worse and worse. He couldn't get out of bed and walk anymore. I had called my best friend from second grade to come and see my dad and to be there for me, but she refused. That really hurt me. She said she couldn't handle seeing it.

Just before Dad went into the hospital, he sold his Lincoln car. I think he knew then that he wasn't going to last long. That Lincoln car was his baby. He was so proud of that car. He had never owned anything that nice his entire life, and even though it was used, it had a sunroof and push buttons and was a complete luxury for him. I took it to prom. It was so big and long; it was like a boat. The high school that he attended had also closed their doors after so many years, and that broke my dad's heart.

My daughter was two and had learned her ABCs and 123s and was so proud to show her grandpica, as she called him. He was so proud of her. He also took pride in a good appearance, especially since he was a salesman. He would try and shave but just couldn't do it, so he would blame the shaver for not working right, but it was that he had become too weak.

It was now that I longed to just see my dad completely alone, without me having to take my daughter, mom and brother with me. I begged my husband to watch our daughter so I could go and be alone with my dad for a little bit. He didn't want to do it but he did. I felt so guilty not taking everyone with me, but I needed this alone time with my dad. I felt like a kid skipping school as I felt I was sneaking out to go see my dad without others knowing it. I just didn't think anyone would understand that I needed to be alone with him. I had went and found out what I was having ahead of time from the ultrasound. I knew I was having a boy, and I wanted to tell my dad.

By now, my baby was kicking and moving around in my belly. I got to the nursing home. It was in the evening. I put my dad's hand on my belly to see if he could feel my baby boy kicking in my belly. This moment in time will never ever be forgotten for me. I was fighting back the tears and trying so hard to be strong for the both of us. My dad had started wetting the bed, and the nurses wouldn't respond. This upset him so much. He begged me to take him home. He wanted to get out of there. I would tell him I would talk to the doctor and would work on it, knowing all along that this was a lie. My heart was so broken now. All those years of my father being such a wonderful man and caregiver to so many and now no one was a caregiver to him. I felt so guilty that I should be doing so much more for him. I felt so helpless.

I continued to go every day to make sure the nurses were changing his bed and that he was taken care of properly. My oldest brother and wife showed up for the decision to place him in the nursing home. They didn't visit him very much. The one day when I visited, the nurse said that my dad kept saying the words, "Thanksgiving Day." They asked me what that meant, and I said that is when my baby was due. He wanted to live until then to see his grandson.

He had stopped eating almost everything. It was the season of fresh peaches. On my way to see him, I stopped at a fresh market stand in a parking lot and picked some up. I took them with me to see dad. I would slice and peel and deseed them and feed them to him. He loved them. They were the only thing he would eat. I was the only one he would eat them for as well.

He had still been working, selling grease and oil, until he was admitted into the hospital. I wanted his advice on how to handle his accounts. I wanted to know if I should contact the person who brought him into the business to let him know that my dad could no longer work the business. As I went to ask my dad this question, my dad became very restless and upset and he wouldn't answer me. I just dropped the subject and tried to calm him down and told him I would take care of it. I felt so bad that I had upset him. I felt so alone. My father was always my go-to person and now I found myself having to make all of these huge decisions on my own. I was growing up superfast with only being in my twenties. I didn't like being an adult.

My father had become pretty much skin and bone now. He had lost so much weight. He had gout pain in his big toes so badly that he couldn't even have the sheets touching his feet. It was now that he pretty much couldn't even talk to us anymore. Each day he kept getting worse before my eyes. It was the hardest thing I had ever had to watch. From the time he was put in the nursing home, he went downhill fast. From the old man shuffle when he walked, to not being able to get out of bed, to not being able to shave, to not eating, to not talking anymore.

During this process I do remember one day I felt like maybe there was a little ray of hope when he was still talking with us and very alert and was laughing and giggling. This moment sticks in my mind and kind of haunts me when I look back on it because dad never really giggled. It was very out of character for him and it was as if it was a cover up for the immense fear of dying that he was facing but didn't want to express.

This had become so hard for all of us that no one felt safe in discussing how any of us were truly feeling about it. I felt I was forced into burying my feelings and emotions because I had to be the strong one now for everyone, and I felt so weak and my heart was aching so badly.

On Saturday, September 3, 1994, only two weeks after being put in the nursing home, my aunt (my dad's sister and only sibling) went and visited my dad by herself. I had been there earlier with my daughter, mom, and brother. I had planned on going back a little later. While at home, my in-laws were over and my husband was next door getting drunk. I had already took my mom and brother home.

My phone was located in the kitchen. I was standing in the kitchen when that dreaded ring came from the phone. I picked it up, and it was the nursing home telling me my dad was gone. They asked me if I wanted to come down to see him before they did anything. I said yes. I told them I would be right down there and to wait for me. I then talked to my aunt. She told me she was by his side while he died and that she told him it was okay to go and listed all the people he would see when he got to heaven. I had felt so guilty once again that I was not there by his side. I was so glad my aunt was there and he did not die alone.

I look back now, and it probably worked out this way for a reason. I don't think I would have been strong enough to let my dad go right before my eyes. It would have been too hard for me and for my dad both. My aunt said that there really wasn't any reason to come back down, so I said okay. I thought about it and decided I couldn't handle seeing him like that anyway, so I called the nursing home back and told them to go ahead with everything and that I didn't need to come down. I hung up the phone, and my in-laws hugged me in the kitchen while I was crying. I had no idea what I was going to do now. I was so numb and so devastated. Then it occurred to me. I had to bury my emotions again and be strong.

I had to go out now and tell my mom and my brother. How was I ever going to tell my brother? He followed my dad everywhere. He was like my dad's bodyguard. He would even go into his room at night to make sure he was still breathing. He was going to be such a lost little puppy dog now.

We had my brother tested, and in some areas he was very smart. He knows all of the capitals to all of the states and is great at board games but lacks common sense. He is at a five-year-old level with common sense and needs a lot of verbal reminders. They said that if you ever need to tell him something important, you have to make it very brief with as few words as possible because he will hear the first thing you say and will be so busy comprehending what you just said that he can't hear anything you say after that.

My mother-in-law went next door to get my husband, her son, home since I needed him. My father-in-law went too and dragged his butt back into the house. He was so drunk. He was falling over and stumbled over his words. He didn't hug me, say he was sorry, or showed any compassion whatsoever. He only became very loud and demanded that he was going to drive me to my mom's. He was now trying to be the man and the hero that was coming to save the day.

At this point, I was so disgusted. He was not helping me. He was only adding more stress to me. I just wanted to drive myself because he was drunk and couldn't drive. I had just gotten the phone call and I had to let my mom and brother know, and now I had to deal with a drunk husband too. Come on already!

My in-laws stayed to take care of my daughter while I had to ride with my husband to my mom's. He would not reason with me when I said I would drive. His parents were not much help with this either. Now I was worried the whole ride out to my mom's since I didn't know if I would get there safely.

When we got there, I barely got into the door when my husband said he would deal with my brother. He just came out with it, "Your dad is dead." It was so cold and the whole thing bothered me, but looking back, it was probably for the best. My brother understood what my husband said because it was very few words, so he could process it. My mom, brother, and older brother seemed to understand.

This was Saturday evening and Monday was Labor Day. I recalled how everything looked around me when I was driving to the nursing home to see my dad for the last time. I saw the sun shining, the construction on the roads, the feel of summer leaving and autumn sweeping in. A change was occurring and one I was just not ready for. My mom and brothers were now my new responsibility to take care of. My heart was so heavy now and ached so badly. I was numb and just going through the motions. I was in a complete fog.

Now, for the funeral arrangements. The day came when we had to go to the funeral home. My parents did have their plots and stones bought and which funeral home to go to, but that was it. We were led up into a room that had a whole bunch of caskets. I had never seen anything like this before, and the whole thing was terrifying for me. We had to walk through this maze of caskets everywhere and try and decide which one to pick. This was the most morbid and disturbing thing I think I have ever done.

This was the hardest thing for me to do. I felt so weak. I just couldn't picture my dad in this creepy box. How in the world was I supposed to pick one of these? I didn't want to pick any. My dad didn't belong there. My dad should still be alive. I couldn't put him in that thing and have him go into the ground. What were these people thinking? I'm supposed to shop for a casket as if I am at a car dealership buying a new car? What the heck? This was morbid as hell and I just wanted out of there! I felt like I was going to faint. We somehow made a decision.

After leaving the room, I excused myself to the bathroom and had diarrhea. I thought I was going to puke. I tried to pull myself together and went back out to finish the other plans. I swore to myself that I would have all my funeral arrangements done ahead of time because I never wanted my children to ever go through this terrifying experience. It was bad enough that I lost my dad, let alone make these kinds of decisions. All I could do was picture my dad rotting in the ground with worms all around him.

After the plans were finally finished, we all went to a local restaurant. I just sat there completely numb. I didn't want to eat anything. How in the heck did they expect me to eat? What is wrong with everyone? Why don't these people understand this is not a party for me? I was not okay! I was not okay at all. I was not okay with any of it! My life would never be the same again. I wasn't ready for any of this. All these thoughts would overflow in my mind as I just sat there going through all the motions.

I thought of my children now and how my daughter was only two and would probably never remember her grandpica. My son would never meet him. How can my children be deprived of such a wonderful person in their lives? My head was hurting, and my thoughts were racing. I just felt sick all over. I was a complete and utter mess; however, no one could tell from the outside. I put on the brave front and swallowed all my emotions like the good person I was supposed to be. I was the caregiver and the strong one. And above all, whatever I did, don't show any of your true emotions to your husband. There would be no sympathy there. I had learned quickly to hide my emotions. I couldn't trust anyone. I felt so alone and isolated now. I had no one to turn to.

The time of the viewing came, and I was holding up. My dad did look better in the casket than he did at the nursing home. I decided I wanted my dad to have one artificial pink rose to hold that said grandpica on it from my daughter. They would always feed my dad's fish together when we went out there. He loved his fish in the pond. I went home and got some fish food pellets and put them in a Ziploc bag to take back to the funeral home and tuck them in my dad's hands. That way, someday, my daughter and her grandpica could feed the fish together again. My parents liked pink roses. That is why I picked pink.

I was at home now and getting myself ready to go to the store to find an artificial pink rose. I was in the bathroom when my heart started racing and it wouldn't stop. My lips were becoming numb, and I was getting pale when I looked in the mirror. I called my next-door neighbor to come over and stay with me.

I was home alone because my husband was at work. Mind you, I was going through funeral proceedings while I was pregnant and my husband decided to work. Of course he does. It was the weekend and Labor Day weekend at that, so it was double and triple time. He couldn't miss that. Who cares that your wife's father just died.

I started having contractions now, and we called for an ambulance. My neighbor stayed with me until the ambulance came, and she called my husband at work. They had got me into the ambulance, and someone I knew was on the run with me. The workers kept saying I should try and breathe, but I couldn't. I remember them on the radio to the emergency room, and I heard panic in everyone's voices. I don't remember much of the ride after that.

Once I was in the hospital, I had doctors and nurses swarming all over me. I had the ER doctor, the heart doctor, the baby doctor, and tons of nurses with all of the EMS people. The contractions were getting worse, my heart was still racing, and I couldn't breathe. They found my heart was racing over two hundred beats per minute. My baby was not getting enough oxygen, which was why I was having contractions. My baby wasn't due for another three months.

I remember everyone screaming stand by. I knew from TV shows that those words were not good. They injected this medicine in me to stop my heart and to start it back up again in hopes that it would start beating at the right pace again. When that happened, I remember I could feel my blood stop flowing and my legs became paralyzed and I was in excruciating pain. I remember just screaming, "My legs, my legs, my legs! What is wrong with my legs!"

When my heart started back up, it was still racing. Now they had to do it again, but at a higher dose this time. This would stop my heart for a longer time and make it riskier to start back up, let alone back up at the right beat. I dreaded hearing them say it didn't take. They told me they were doing it again. I didn't want my legs to hurt again, but they did it, so my legs did it again. Then they all of a sudden screamed, "It worked!"

By this time, my husband was just arriving. I was still having contractions, so I had to drink this really bad tasting green liquid to stop the contractions. It worked. Just as all of this was happening, a young male doctor with reddish short hair came up to me and said, "Remember when you came in, I told you my name was Ralph." I said no. This time he was right in my face and said, "Remember when you came in, I told you my name was Ralph."

I looked at him funny. He backed off then and said, "I am just joking. My name is Jeff." I looked at him like what the heck. I thought he was joking around with me and knew my dad just died because my dad's name was Ralph. I thought, "How sick can someone be?" He saw my disgusted look on my face and asked what was wrong and if I know someone named Ralph.

I said, "Yes, that is my dad and he just died." He said he was so sorry and walked away. I knew then that the guy was not joking around. It hit me right there that that was my dad in the ER with me. My husband was next to me, and I kept saying, "That was my dad. That was my dad." My husband kept trying to make me stop saying that because I was embarrassing him and he didn't believe me. He thought I was nuts, so I stopped. I had thought at first the person I knew on the EMS had said something to the doctor that my dad had just died, but she didn't. I later asked her if she remembered Dr. Jeff and she hadn't remembered him at all.

They decided to admit me. What was I going to do? My dad's funeral was the next day. What about my mom and brothers? I called my oldest brother and told him what happened, where I was, and that I couldn't get mom and the other brothers to the funeral home so he would have to do it. I also told him I wanted a pink rose with grandpica on it and have that put in my dad's hands. I told him not to tell my mom and brothers that I was in the hospital. I didn't want them to know and worry about me when they had enough to deal with already.

By the time they got me all settled into a room, it was getting dark out. My husband came to the room with us when they got me settled. Lying there, a huge flood of fear came over me. My dad had died. My baby and I almost died. I was terrified. I begged and pleaded with my husband to stay the night with me and to not leave my side, but with absolutely no emotion whatsoever, he said he had to get home and go to bed because he was tired. He left me all alone, while he did not think anything of it.

I started sobbing. I was all alone and scared. My mind was racing again. What am I going to do? I have a drunk, uncompassionate husband, a two-year-old, a baby in my belly, a disabled mom and two brothers to take care of. I just lost my dad who was the one I always went to and not a single friend or person I could talk to or depend on or trust now. My whole life was unraveling right before me, and I couldn't do anything about it. I was curled up in a fetal position, sobbing uncontrollably in my own grief and fear, all alone. I was completely and totally *all* alone. This was the lowest point of my entire life. I literally cried myself to sleep.

I prayed and begged God to please be with me now. In that moment, I had ten huge stresses of life I had to deal with all at the same time.

- My dad died, and I'm completely alone with no one by my side.
- I had to take care of my mom who was disabled.
- I had to take care of my brother who is disabled.
- I had to take care of a second brother who is disabled.
- I was pregnant.
- I had a two-year-old daughter to take care of.
- I was just sick with my heart racing.
- I almost just died.
- My baby almost died.
- And the rejection from my husband.

No wonder I can't remember this time in my life. The Lord was saying, nope. She is done. Not one more thing. I will block her memory.

When my baby doctor came in to see me, he wanted to know why I was even there at the hospital. I told him about my heart and my dad dying and my stress and how my dad was in the emergency room with me. He disregarded everything and simply said, "You can't be stressed because your baby will turn out to be gay." Also, at one of my doctor's appointments, he asked if I was from the Mediterranean because I had a brown line going from my belly button to my pelvic area on my skin. He said women from the Mediterranean have that dark line on their belly. He was not a nice person. He did not have a good bedside manner at all.

The next day arrives, and it is my dad's funeral. Everything now is a complete blur to me. I only can remember bits and pieces of this day, even now. I don't know if the doctors gave me drugs to make me not remember or if God only gives you as much as you can handle and so He blocked things out because I wouldn't be able to handle it. Either way, I don't know how I got to the funeral home from the hospital. I don't know how I got dressed. My mom and brothers got there. I assume my oldest brother must have taken them. I remember my mother-in-law hugging me saying she didn't know I had a heart problem. Then I heard people whispering, "She is not all right. She has lost so much weight." My teacher from high school was there.

All of my dad's classmates were there in a section of their own on the side. My dad was the first to die from his high school class. There were around ten in the class, and they all still got together. Three in the class were all cousins, my dad and two others.

I remember placing the fish food in my dad's hand the day before. I also noticed the pink rose that I asked my brother for was also there. I remember being in the kitchen and not wanting to walk out in front of everyone to take a seat. They said I got up and talked. I do not remember this at all. I don't remember anything else. I don't remember who else was there or who I talked to or what I did or what happened. I don't remember the cemetery at all. I vaguely remember being at our church for food and my daughter was playing in the churchyard with my best friend and her mom.

I do remember that at my mom's home after the funeral, she was giving away the plants and flowers that were given to me. I was upset because I wanted to keep them. I do not recall which preacher was at my mom's house, but I do remember him saying that this chapter is now over and you must start a new chapter with your life. My best friend from second grade agreed with him the whole way. These words are true, don't get me wrong, but these were not the words I needed to hear right then. This came across as very cold and mean hearted. It sounded like "Get over it already." We just put my dad in the ground for crying out loud! I am supposed to be okay with all of this because it is over? How cruel can these people be?

Maybe they didn't know my dad as well as I did or loved him like I did, but come on already. Maybe they can say this and move on without any problems, but I couldn't. They expected me to just say oh well. I wasn't even crying, that I remember, for them to say these hurtful words in order to coax me to stop crying. They didn't want me to mourn then or even later, and I was just still in shock from everything. I just got out of the hospital and was in a complete fog and not feeling loved by anyone. It felt like no one cared, and I felt all alone again. My mom didn't even seem fazed that he was gone. What was wrong with everyone?

No one even asked me if I was okay. Maybe I don't want to start a new chapter right now. Maybe I don't want all of these new responsibilities. Maybe I am not all right with this and maybe I don't want any of this. It is easy for others to say this. They are not the ones who have to go through this. Where was any love, caring, compassion, or sympathy for me right now? None. Absolutely none, nowhere to be found. No, I was just supposed to slap a big smile on my face and take the world on my shoulders and just be happy and thrilled about the whole damn thing. What the heck was wrong with everyone?

People can be so mean. I never felt so alone in all my life. I was falling into great despair with no one to catch me. I wanted to say, "Screw all of you." I wanted to just be left alone. I didn't even know what was going on, let alone accept it. No one will ever understand how deep my scars went and how deeply hurt I was from this. How people I thought I could love and trust had turned on me at the worst time of my life and not just one person we are talking about. I felt like everyone, no matter where I turned at that time, was not there for me. It all seemed to happen at the same time when I needed someone, anyone, the most. I was so very alone with my grief. No wonder I can't remember most of this very, very, very traumatic time in my life. Later, I realized this was when the Lord was carrying me. I went back to the hospital emergency room after the funeral to talk to Dr. Jeff that was with me in the emergency room. I asked for him, and they told me there has never been a doctor named Jeff that worked there. I knew from that moment on that Jeff was an angel sent by God to tell me my dad was okay.

I turned to God. He was the only one I had. I would pray and talk to Him. I would open up the Bible and just turn to any page, and He would talk to me and answer me every time from the page I had turned to.

'In all their affliction He was afflicted, And the Angel of His Presence saved them; In His love and in His pity He redeemed them; And He bore them and carried them All the days of old.' (Isaiah 63:9).

He didn't take my problems away or the pain, but He gave me strength and endurance to keep putting one foot in front of the other. He helped me keep breathing, moving, and living. I realized the Lord didn't want me to live in fear like I had been my whole life. I realized I was never alone and never would be. I did not need to be afraid.

"'For I, the Lord your God, will hold your right hand, saying to you, 'Fear not, I will help you.'" (Isaiah 41:13).

"Be strong and of good courage, do not fear nor be afraid of them; for the Lord your God, He is the One who goes with you. He will not leave you nor forsake you." (Deuteronomy 31:6).

I want to pause here for a moment. If you are going through any kind of loss, rejection, loneliness, worry, or fear, I want to offer you hope. Take a leap of faith and reach out to Jesus. Faith is not from the brain but from the heart. Jesus and God are very real.

"Trust in the Lord with all your heart, And lean not on your own understanding; In all your ways acknowledge Him, And He shall direct your paths." (Proverbs 3:5-6).

If you have not accepted Jesus as your Savior and you would like to, please say this prayer.

Dear Lord Jesus, I believe you were born from the Virgin Mary. I believe you suffered and died on the cross and you shed your precious blood to save my sins. I believe you rose again to heaven, and I accept you as my Savior. I am a sinner, and I need your forgiveness. Please forgive me of my sins and come dwell in my heart so that I can walk in obedience with you and be with you in heaven when I die, forever and ever. In Jesus's name I pray. Amen!

If you said this prayer and meant it with your heart, believing in Jesus, accepting Jesus as your Savior, confessing and repenting of your sins, and willing to walk in obedience to Him with His help, you are saved. He will always be with you to help you.

As days went by, I remember being bombarded with tons of paperwork. Now being the attorney in fact over everyone, I had to deal with the nursing home, the funeral home, the will, the lawyers, the social security, the hospital, the doctors, the bank, the bills, prescriptions. The list just went on and on and on. No one could have prepared me for all of this. You don't learn this stuff in school. I was being forced into a crash course and had to grow up in a heartbeat. Paperwork, paperwork, paperwork.

I remember being in the grocery store and seeing peaches. Out of nowhere, right in the middle of the store, I started crying. It all came flooding back to me when I fed dad the peaches while he was in his bed. This mourning process was all new to me. I learned quickly that you could be going along for a while and then all of a sudden, out of nowhere, this overwhelming feeling of grief attacks you. I went through this for a very long time.

I remember when my husband and I went on a boat ride with friends on a lake and how the sun was shining and it was late afternoon going into evening and how the sky looked and how you could tell summer was on the brink of leaving and fall was approaching fast. My heart was so heavy. I missed my dad so much, and my life was never going to be the same again. I sat there quietly. I had nothing to say while everyone else was having a good time. I just couldn't, even if I tried. I was so numb with pain. That time of year and how the sky and sun looked haunt me to this day.

At Halloween, I was on a bowling team. I painted my pregnant tummy to look like a jack-o'-lantern. Everyone loved it.

Thanksgiving Day came and went, and I was still pregnant. We had an ultrasound done, and he was sucking his thumb in my belly. I still have the ultrasound picture of this. When I was little, I sucked the last three fingers on my right hand. He must have gotten this from me. He was content staying put. My belly was huge. I had skinny stick arms and legs and this huge belly that looked like I was going to fall over. I couldn't drive because my belly was in the way of the steering wheel. I could no longer carry a laundry basket full of clothes either. I became too top heavy and it felt like I was going to fall over.

Two weeks after Thanksgiving, which was my due date, I finally had him on December 4, 1994. It was a Sunday. I had went in around midnight and had him at 5:56 a.m. He was 8 lbs. 7 ¼ oz. and 20 ½ inches long. They had to break my water. He had ingested some, so they had to work on him to get the fluids out.

My hips were too small to push him out, and when I did, he pushed my hip right out of the socket, and I had to have my hip put back in. Needless to say, Lamaze breathing totally went out the window. You don't think a pound bigger makes much of a difference, but when it is coming out down there, you better believe it honey, it's huge! At one point, I said, "Lord, please help me." My husband became upset because I was embarrassing him.

My baby boy had quite a bit of dark, straight long hair and lots of baby rolls. He had a round face with chubby cheeks and a little nose and mouth. His skin complexion was darker than my daughter's. He had blue eyes as well and ten fingers and ten toes. He was a healthy bouncing baby boy.

When I held him, I had such strong mixed emotions. I was so happy he was alive and well, but I was also so sad because my dad was not there to see him. It was such a bittersweet moment. I remembered my prayer from my freshman year of high school and how I asked the Lord to keep my dad alive at least until I was married and for him to see my firstborn, and the Lord answered that prayer. My father was now looking over me, my new son, my daughter, my mother, and my brothers.

My mom came to the hospital to hold my baby boy and my in-laws were there too. My husband was there and brought our daughter. With everything that was going on, I think I failed in preparing my daughter about what happens after the baby in my belly was born. We tried to get our daughter to hold her baby brother and she did, but she was not happy about it at all.

On our way home from the hospital, I had to sit in the backseat in the middle. We had the baby in the one car seat and our daughter in the other. Our daughter was so upset that this baby or thing was in our car with us. She thought this baby, once out of my belly, was staying at the hospital. It was certainly *not* coming home with us. She tried to crawl out of her car seat the whole way home. She was crying and screaming and all upset. She kept trying to reach for the car door handle while we were going down the road. I literally had to hold her down in her car seat the whole way home. Once we got home and everyone got settled, we sat down with our daughter and explained everything to her. She finally calmed down and eventually learned to accept it. She grew to love him, and they have a very special bond today.

It was December now, and our church was putting on a little program for Christmastime. They had asked me if I would dress up like Mary and hold my baby boy, only a couple of weeks old, as baby Jesus. I agreed to do it. This is one decision I will never regret making. This is a very special memory for me. I will never forget this moment. They had me dress up like Mary, and I had my baby wrapped in a blanket and was holding him in my arms. They had me sit on a seat, near the altar, in front of the congregation. I never had to say a word. The preacher did all the readings and songs were sung.

I remember "Away in a Manger" and "Silent Night" and how the lights were dim. I just sat there holding my baby boy, who was sleeping the whole time, looking down at him and feeling so honored to be playing this role. I can never describe the way I felt. So much joy that my baby boy was alive and well, and safe and sound in my arms. I felt so much love, safety, and peace in those moments that I was holding him. I did not want this moment to ever end. I cherished this moment then, and I still cherish that moment today. I can say that was a God moment.

New Year's Eve came, and of course, my husband wanted to go out with friends and get drunk. I just wanted to stay home. I was not in the party mood. I was missing my dad, but once again it didn't matter what I wanted or how I felt, I had to go along. The in-laws had our kids. When we got there, I was very quiet. I didn't want to be there. The friends kept asking me what my problem was. They thought I should be happy and partying. It never occurred to any of them that I was just now getting to my grief and mourning. I didn't want the year of 1994 to end. This was the year my dad was still alive in. I didn't want to say good-bye to this year. It had only been four months since my dad had died. I was not ready to close this chapter yet. Why, why, why? Is everyone trying to deprive me of grieving for my father? Damn it, damn it, damn it! What was wrong with everyone? I tried so hard to get through the night and tried so hard to keep the tears at bay.

Then midnight hit and this huge amount of grief swelled up inside of me as I was slow dancing to "Auld Lang Syne." These words mean "old long ago." It is about love and friendship in times past. "Should auld acquaintance be forgot, and never brought to mind? Should auld acquaintance be forgot, and auld lang syne! For auld lang syne, my dear, for auld lang syne. We'll take a cup o' kindness yet, for auld lang syne."

The words, to me, meant I was supposed to forget about my dad and his love for me and how I felt everyone wanted me to do just that, and I just couldn't. I couldn't hold back my tears any longer. I ended up leaving and going to the bathroom. I wanted the frick out of there. I felt so trapped. The girl friends wondered what my problem was, and when I started to mention my dad, they all thought I was so ridiculous. They snubbed me and they went back off to their drinking and partying that they had to do so badly. No, no, no compassion, not even one ounce of compassion towards me at all! I was so alone in my pain.

Later in the summer, my husband and I decided to take our first family trip with the kids alone, just the four of us. We decided to go to Sea World. It was so neat to see the whale and dolphins and the shows. I had never been there and I thought it was really cool. Our son carried a blue baby blanket around with him everywhere and would suck his thumb. At the Shamu whale show, they had a big-screen TV set. They captured our son, in the audience, on the big screen, sucking his thumb and holding his blanket. They thought he was so cute. I tried to take a picture of the screen. I think I have that picture around somewhere. My husband and I hardly even said two words to each other the entire trip. He didn't want to be there. He was making it miserable for all of us. Not only was this our first family trip, it was our last. The one and only family trip we took together.

We planned a baptism for our son on October 8, 1995, Sunday. We had also planned to have a party at our house afterward to celebrate with family and friends and to have cake. My husband, the night before on Saturday, decided to stay up all night and get drunk. By the time of the baptism, and the party afterward, my husband was still very drunk and hung over. He embarrassed me so much in front of my family. I was so upset with him.

All he did was work six days a week. He would take Saturday off and work Sunday for double time. He would work all the holidays for the triple time. The one day he did have off a week, he would either hunt, fish, drink, or gamble. He never spent any time with me and the kids. We lived our own separate lives away from him. He didn't want anything to do with us. He expected me to have his laundry done, food bought, food prepared, dishes done, and his house cleaned. I was not a wife. I was his slave and mother. I felt he wanted a single bachelor life with a housekeeper or maid, and didn't want a wife, children, and a family.

We would sometimes get household items together at the store, but that was about it. I would take the kids to church and visit relatives by myself or go to the fair, festivals, fireworks, parades, to see

Santa or the Easter Bunny, trick or treating, and shopping all by myself with our kids.

When my daughter was playing outside one summer, we had some baby kittens under our shed. She was over by the shed to check them out. We had railroad ties for landscaping boarders. A swarm of hornets had made a home in the ties. She was walking on the boarder by the shed when she stepped on the swarm, making them mad, and they flew up under her clothes and she got stung multiple times. I saw her running, falling, and crying. I grabbed her up and stripped her clothes off and made sure all of the hornets were gone, but she had already been stung several times. We went inside, and I tried to treat her and watched her closely. I noticed she started swelling really fast. So I called the ambulance.

Our local chief of police, who was my great friend, came to the house. She got there first and stayed with us until the ambulance got there. My son was about six months old and was sleeping in his crib. When they got there, they gave her an Epi-Pen right away to stop the swelling. The swelling had gotten to her face and was starting to swell her throat. Fortunately, they got there fast enough and got the medicine in her quickly, so the swelling went down before she was not able to breathe.

I grabbed my son and my purse and rode in the front of the ambulance while my daughter was in the back. They were so nice to her and kept talking to her to keep her calm. They gave her a blue stuffed animal teddy bear, and she still has that today. They checked her all over when we got to the hospital, and she was okay, so we were able to go home. A guy who was friends with us heard about it and came over right away. He had stuff with him to kill the hornets. He was able to kill them all.

One time when I was cleaning my daughter's bedroom closet, she was in another part of the house. For some reason, she took my fingernail clippers from the bathroom, threw them in the trash can in the kitchen, and took off with the trash can outside into the backyard, over to the backyard of our neighbor next door, and into an empty field on the other side next to them and left my blue plastic kitchen trash can in the field. She came back home and came back in the house.

I needed my fingernail clippers and noticed they were missing and I had no idea where they went. Then I noticed the trash can was gone. I found that really weird. How can a trash can just up and disappear? It was pretty good sized. Then we had to go run some errands and I drove by the field and noticed a blue trash can in the field. I thought that was odd, still not thinking it was mine. How could my trash can get out there?

After going home, and not being able to find my trash can anywhere, I walked over to the field to look at the blue trash can that was there. Sure enough, it was mine and there were my fingernail clippers inside it. I asked my daughter if she did that, and she said yes. I asked her why, and she had no idea why she did it. I guess she was bored. She was young at the time. She got in trouble for going outside without me knowing about it.

Another time, she got in trouble was when we got done eating at Wendy's and she was going to open the door and dart out into the parking lot with cars coming and not staying by my side and holding my hand. She got yelled at the whole way home on that one and she never did that again. I was strict when it came to safety and behaving the right way in public. Before getting out of our car, I would go over all the rules every time so they wouldn't forget. Being mostly a single mom with no help, they had to follow my orders.

There was this other time when I was in the kitchen doing dishes and the kids were playing. My daughter was teaching my son how to play hide and seek. My son didn't quite understand that you close your eyes and count so that my daughter could hide. He didn't want to close his eyes. So my daughter thought if she put him in the bathroom but locked the door first, before shutting it, that would work. She asked him if he could unlock the door and get out, and he said yes. She didn't think that was good enough, so to make sure she could hide, she put him in the dryer and closed the dryer door. She asked him if he could open it and he said "yes." She left him in the dryer, locked the bathroom door, shut it behind her, and then went to hide.

While I was still doing dishes, I heard a faint yell, "Mommy help!" I couldn't figure out where it was coming from at first. Then I knew it was the bathroom with the washer and dryer in it. I went to open the door, but it was locked. I asked my daughter where her brother was, and she said in the bathroom. I asked why the door was locked, and she told me everything and then said he was in the dryer. I was like what! She repeated herself, and so I panicked. You did *what?* Now I was really trying to get the door unlocked, and I couldn't get it. My husband was at work. I went next door, and the neighbor man came over and got the door unlocked for me. I was able then to open the dryer door and get my son out. My daughter got into trouble for that one too. My son was okay, thank goodness.

Chapter 21

HELL! DID I MENTION I WAS IN HELL YET?!

My husband wanted to go and get a tattoo. I didn't want to go or have anything to do with it, so I stayed home. As time started to pass that evening, I got in the car and went to the party to try and stop him from getting a tattoo. Once I got there, all the girls were getting one and were trying to convince me to get one. I broke down and started looking in the book. They had teddy bears. I was collecting them at the time, so it caught my eye. With a little more persuading, I broke down and had one done. I had it put on my right arm just above my wrist. I had picked the teddy bear with blue eyes because both my daughter and son had blue eyes. It was holding a pink rose because my mom and dad liked pink roses and I had my daughter and son's names put on the top and bottom of the teddy bear. It turned out very nice, but I regretted it right after I did it and even tried to see how much it would cost to remove it. It would have been very expensive and would have left a scar, so I didn't remove it.

I was so sorry to Jesus and never had another one. I covered it for quite a while. I know the Lord has forgiven me. I never did stop my husband for getting one. He got one on his upper arm of the grim reaper. From that moment on, he changed completely. He went from bad to much, much worse. Evil flowed from him. It was like he was marked by the devil. He went on to get three more tattoos later. One was a dragon looking like it was busting out of his skin on the other upper arm. On one side of his chest he got one of a yin and yang circle and the other side a picture of our son and daughter.

He had his drinking buddies over. He got really drunk, got on the four-wheeler, and drove it really fast in our driveway. He ran it into the side of our house by the garage. It put tire marks on the siding and bent the siding all up. Then the town was doing some work next to our house with a backhoe. Why the town left the keys in it was beyond me. Well, my husband decided, while drunk, to get on it and start it up. It was at night, and his friends were there. He started pushing all kinds of buttons, and the arm with the scoop begun swinging all over and he kept banging it up and down. I thought he was going to get it tangled into the electrical lines. He was making so much noise I thought the neighbors would hear and see and then call the cops on us. I begged him to stop, but he wouldn't listen. You can't argue with a drunk.

One night, the weather was really bad outside. It was wintertime, and the roads were nothing but ice. We met another couple at the movies at a town about forty-five minutes away. My husband had been drinking and was very drunk, so I drove home. I couldn't go very fast or would spin out. This made my husband mad because he wanted me to go at least fifty-five mph and I couldn't. He threatened to hit me if I didn't go as fast as he wanted me to. Here I was stuck in that all too familiar hard spot. I was stuck with either taking the risk of an accident or getting beat up. My body was shaking so badly. When we finally got home and in the garage, he appeared to be passed out. I was so mad I called him an asshole. He was only pretending to be passed out, however, and heard what I called him. He started threatening me again. I got out of the vehicle, got the kids, and took off outside with them. I hid behind the neighbor's shed until I thought it was finally safe to go home.

My best friend from second grade was now a flight attendant. I flew with her to New York for the day. I had never been there before. It was so big and impressive. We drove under the buildings and then you were surrounded by so many big skyscrapers you felt like you were inside. It was Christmastime, and we went to the Trump Tower. It was decorated with a tall tree and a huge wreath all lit up and had a wall that was a water fountain. We went into a very expensive store. We didn't buy anything, just looked. We stayed away from Time

Square because they said it was kind of dangerous there. We did go to Rockefeller Center, the Empire State Building, walked past the World Trade Center, and saw the Statue of Liberty from a distance.

We then went on another trip together to Tampa, Florida. We drove along the ocean. It was nice but we were supposed to meet my aunt and uncle who lived down there in the winter. They had supper all ready for us but we never were able to show up. My friend was driving a rent-a-car and we kept getting lost, so we never made it there. I was extremely mad. My aunt wasn't too happy about it either.

By this last trip, my friend's mother confronted me about a past secret of her daughters and wanted me to tell her the truth about it. At that time, we both felt she needed help and were concerned for her. Her mother wanted the truth so she could try to reach out and help her daughter, so I told her the truth. I didn't say anything to my friend because I felt like I was walking on eggshells around her. I was always there for her, but she wasn't there for me. I felt if she knew I told her mom the truth, then she would never speak to me again.

My husband and I decided to go on another houseboat trip with a group of people again. Some of the people were the same and some different. At this point, our marriage was not doing well at all. I sensed something not right with my husband. Another couple on the trip was my ex-boyfriend and his wife. We were friends again at this point. My husband kept flirting with my ex-boyfriend's wife to make me jealous. I tried to pull him away to have alone time with him in the hot tub. Others were trying to support me. Little did I know that everyone on the boat, except for me, knew that he was having an affair. The affair was with someone other than the one he was flirting with. The one he was having an affair with was not on the boat with us. He did go to the hot tub with me, and we tried to bond with no success.

We had a trip to Vegas scheduled for quite a long time. By the time it was time to go on the trip, my husband did not want to go, that is, with me. He wanted to go to Vegas with her. We ended up going together. I remember telling my husband on the plane we can make this work and he would agree by mouth, but his actions always said otherwise. The first night we got there, all he wanted to do was gamble at the tables and then got really drunk. I wanted no part of this. I ended up eating by myself. I would go down time to time to check on him. I ended up sneaking chips into my pocket without him seeing it. He was so drunk. I left and I guess he passed out down there and got into trouble and lost all our money. He came back to the room and fell into the tub and ripped the shower curtain down and passed out on the bed.

I had put on a very pretty long black dress that was slimming and I looked great. I was trying to get his attention, only for him to criticize me in it. I was 116 pounds, but he said I looked fat. It was a good thing I had the chips because that was all the money we had left for food for the rest of the trip and to get home. We couldn't go to any shows. We did everything free. We walked to all the casinos and saw the free shows. That was about it.

My best friend from second grade, like I mentioned before, was a flight attendant. She eventually found out her mom had asked me about her secret and that I had told her mom the truth. So from that time on, she refused to ever see me, speak to me, or forgive me, even though I tried many times to ask for forgiveness throughout the years.

Coming home from Vegas and being in the airport, the flight attendants reminded me of my best friend and my loss. I also knew deep down this was the end of my marriage. I went into the bathroom of the airport and just lost it. I was crying hysterically in the stall, feeling so alone and lost. Everyone I ever known my whole life and loved dearly was leaving me in one form or another. My father dying, my husband about to leave me for another woman, and my best friend from second grade to not have anything more to do with me. My whole world was crashing down around me from all directions all at one time. I pulled myself together before getting on that plane with my husband to go home. I refused to let him know I had been crying. It was a horrible, horrible time for me in my life.

After we got home, things only continued to escalate and got worse and worse. So many nights now, he had guys over so they could play poker and drink all night long in our garage. It got to where the drinking all night led into going to the bar in the morning when it opened to go drink some more. I would have to hide money in the house because he would spend it all on gambling and drinking and we wouldn't have anything for the bills. I managed all the money, thank goodness for that.

Throughout all of this time, my husband, I believe, was having an affair, but I was still unaware of that at this point. Then I noticed how he couldn't kiss me anymore. Then while doing his laundry, I kept smelling women's perfume on his work T-shirts. The smell made me so nauseous. This is when I started to suspect something. He told me there were rumors going around that he was having an affair with someone at work. As the days went on, I received thirty plus calls from thirty plus different people from all over the county to tell me I could not trust my husband and that he was having an affair and who it was with.

I went to his work and confronted her and I could smell the same perfume on her, so I knew it was all true. I kept one of his T-shirt and underwear with the scent in a Ziploc bag and didn't wash it. I kept this as my proof. I discovered it was White Diamonds Elizabeth Taylor perfume. I would smell it in a store or on someone and immediately got a stomachache.

I tried tracking him down one night to try and catch him but couldn't. Everybody now had known about this but me, and now I knew too. You just don't think it would ever happen to you, and it did. And it hurt. Like hell. He kept saying it was all my fault because I didn't keep his house clean enough and I pushed him away and made him do it. Wow, just wow. The house was a *Better Homes and Gardens* home. I didn't have everything perfect enough like his mom, and I guess he expected me to. The marriage was so doomed. Our views on marriage could not have been more different if you tried. He was in the wrong, but he would never tell the truth and admit what he did or even have any remorse for it. He only blamed me and defended everything he did. I felt he wanted a maid, not a wife. Now that my dad died, I had new responsibilities and being his maid was not one of my big priorities anymore, especially since he was not meeting my needs as a husband.

His drinking kept getting worse. The mental and emotional abuse kept getting worse too. There were so many mind games. He did not respect me as a human, wife, or mother of his children. He would make mean comments in a joking way to his friends in front of me. He would defend himself and say he was just joking, but I knew he wasn't. I knew he really meant what he would say. He made comments like he wanted to kill me and bury me in the backyard. He would not let me see any of my friends or family much and he wouldn't let us do anything with them. We always had to do what he wanted to do with his family and friends. I had to see my family by myself when he wasn't around.

He became very controlling. He would never fully communicate. I first thought it was because he was shy, but he did not know how to communicate properly. You never knew what he was thinking. He became this monster that could not show feelings. He couldn't smile or laugh unless he was drunk, and it was an evil laugh. Not a laugh from joy. He could not feel or show joy. He could not cry or feel or show sadness. He had no compassion or kindness or caring. He had no idea how to love. He was never sorry for anything and never felt he did anything wrong ever. He had no fear. He felt nothing. It was like he was not human at all. His eyes became so evil to look at. His eyes would go right through you from across a room. I could not be in the same room with him anymore. I had to sleep on the couch and could not sleep in the bed with him anymore.

He would drink, be mean, and pass out. He peed one night on the electric baseboard heater on the wall in our bedroom and he made me clean it up. I woke up hearing, *ting, ting, ting,* and screamed at him, "What are you doing?" It smelled so bad every time the heat would come on. It was impossible to clean up.

He would embarrass me in public. He would be so drunk and stumbling over everything, and I would have to hold him up. So many nights, I could not wait until he would pass out so I wouldn't have to deal with him. He kept his guns for hunting in the gun cabinet in our bedroom. This is why I had to sleep on the couch after a while. I had gone through so much mental abuse that I truly wanted my husband dead so I no longer had to put up with it. I even expressed my feelings to my family doctor.

I had saw on one of Oprah's TV shows the twelve steps they go by in AA. I wrote them down. I remember them saying how each person has to be responsible for the twelve steps, even the one who is not the alcoholic, and that I needed to change. I remember being in my bathtub crying my eyes out and so bitter because my husband, his family, and his friends were all so mean to me, but I was the one who was supposed to change. I was the one being hurt. I was the victim, but I have to change? They don't have to change but I do. I didn't understand this at all at the time, and it did not sit well with me at all.

I tried really hard to understand this all and I worked on it. He would pick fights. He would set up obstacles to see me fail. He was not supportive. He would argue about me putting salt and pepper in the wrong shakers when I had it right all along. He just wanted to play mind games and try and mess with my head, to make me think I did something wrong and so he could use this as an excuse to punish me. He always put me in situations where I was backed into a corner with no way out. I was always put between a rock and a hard spot, and no matter which way I turned, it would be wrong and he made sure I paid for it. He deliberately would set these scenarios up to get his thrills. He was very sick and demented. I never went to anyone about any of this. His parents did not know most of this, and I never told my parent about any of it either.

One morning before our daughter left for preschool, she wanted to show her daddy a picture she drew and she was so excited to show him. Instead of her daddy saying how proud he was of her and complimenting her, he pipes up—of course hung over and getting ready to go to work since he worked second shift and our daughter had morning preschool—that he couldn't tell what it was and that it should look a lot better than that, and it broke her heart.

I took our daughter to preschool and tried to reassure her that Mommy loved her picture and that it was fine just the way it was. I was so furious by now. How dare he insult our daughter? It was one thing if he wanted to insult me, but I will be damned if he was going to do this to our daughter. When I got home from dropping her off, our son was in the kitchen with us in his walker. I confronted my husband, and I told him he was never to do that again. He denied everything, and I said, "You are so drunk all the time you don't know anything you do." I told him next time he is drunk and does this stuff, I will have a tape recorder playing and I will play it back to him when he is sober.

He came flying at me, grabbed me by the throat, and threw me up against the kitchen wall. He wouldn't let go, and he was trying to choke and kill me. Our son saw the whole thing and started crying. I very sternly said, "You let go of me right this minute, look what you are doing to our son." After a while, he let go. I told him to go to work, and after he left, I went to the emergency room. He left and I went.

They could tell I was extremely depressed and wanted the whole story of what happened, and I told the whole truth. The cops came to the emergency room, and I had to fill out a report. They were going to arrest him for domestic violence, but it was sent to the police to handle from the town we lived in and that police officer knew us very well and got him off if he agreed to counseling. He agreed only so he didn't have to go to jail. The counseling was a joke. We went one time and didn't have to return, so he got off scot-free. It was soon after this he decided he was moving out. He had been sneaking money behind my back and saving it to move out and file for a dissolution. I wanted a family picture with our dog and two kids. We did get that, but I had one taken with me and my two kids and dog without him as well.

One night, while I was asleep on the couch, I woke up startled. I had the little night lights on. My dog woke up and was growling. Coming out of one of the pictures on the wall was this evil spirit, and it looked like a woman fortuneteller and it kept coming closer and closer to me. My dog was growling fiercely at it now, and I was so terrified. I turned the light fully on, but it only came closer. I covered my head with my covers, and I just kept praying and praying and praying for complete protection and for it to go away. I prayed for all the angels to protect us and for all of my family members who had already passed away. I called out to each one of them to help protect us. I had never been so terrified in my whole life. I had an angel that lit up that you usually put on top of your Christmas tree as a tree topper, but I kept it lit and on the fireplace mantle all year. I kept looking at that for relief. After constant prayer, whatever it was, finally left. I was so shook up about it that I went to my pastor the next day to share my concerns. She said I was under a lot of stress. She didn't believe what I experienced was real at all. She made me think there was something not right with me.

It was getting near the end of the year. My husband confronted me about leaving, and I asked him to wait until after Christmas and he did. I don't think he wanted to wait that long, but he did. The only good thing he did was work and provide an income.

I was on the bowling league around this same time, and they were all very supportive of me and felt bad for me and what I was going through. I remember while hitting the pins, I would hope that somehow this nightmare would go away and that my husband would come back and love me. Bowling was a good distraction, and it got me out of the house and around other people.

We somehow got through the holidays, and then at the first of the year, he moved out. He had his drinking buddies come help him. He got an apartment next to her. It was so convenient for them. They should have just moved in together. They were not fooling anyone.

I went to her apartment and told her what I thought and that breaking up marriage after marriage was wrong. She had a huge history of this at work. I was right in her face and pointing my finger at her face. I never touched her. I just made it very clear in getting my point across. I was more upset knowing how she destroyed all the other marriages as well, not just mine. Her mother called me later to tell me she didn't agree with what her daughter had done but that I was not to confront her in front of her granddaughter. I never even entered that apartment. We both stood at the front door. Her daughter happened to be there. Nothing was said or done that was inappropriate for her daughter to see or hear except the truth of her mother. If she didn't want her to know her dirty little secret and lies, then she shouldn't have done them in the first place.

When he moved out, he took the rocker recliner, his guns and cabinet, hunting stuff, his deer head, the kitchen table and chairs, the riding lawn mower, both jet skis and his truck. He took his twin bed and dresser with his clothes, then off he went. It was so hard to get through but a relief as well. It was something that had to be done.

Since he took the table and chairs, his mother bought another set for me and the kids to have. She didn't like that I was using my patio table and chairs as my kitchen table and chairs. I was the one with the big lawn and no mower to mow it with. He didn't even have a yard, but he took the mower. I went shopping for a riding lawn mower by myself, and I did very well, if I do say so myself. I got the mower home and mowed the backyard while screaming the song "Victory in Jesus" at the top of my lungs over and over and over again. I was getting the anger out, my pain out, and it put a smile on my face and a giggle knowing the Lord had my back and that I was going to be okay. I'm a fighter and a survivor. I faced my fears and started doing things on my own that I never did before because I thought I needed a man to do these things.

One thing I started doing was grilling outside. He also took the grill, so I went out and bought a little charcoal grill, charcoal, lighter fluid, and some hamburger patties. I set everything up in the backyard. I was always afraid of the lighter fluid and starting a fire, so I had never done it. I always had the men in my life do it. I decided to face my fear and do this myself. I arranged the charcoal, put the lighter fluid on and got ready to light it and jump back if I had to. I held my breath then lit it. It lit and then I had the flame, and it did what it was supposed to by burning the charcoal. I had never felt so alive and proud of myself as I did in that moment. It sounds silly and simple and crazy, but I had faced my fear! I could do it without a man, and this was a *huge* revelation for me. I never felt so revitalized. It was a sign and a special symbol and special moment for me to know I was going to be okay in all areas of life, and this was just the first step in my new life.

I also planned a long car trip for myself to go visit my cousin in Huntington, West Virginia. I had never read a map and done anything like this before by myself. I had a very fun, successful, and safe trip, and was learning so much about myself now. I also went on a bus tour that took us to a casino boat. I played the slots and walked away with my trip all paid for and some extra money to boot. With my husband keeping me from my family all those years, the trip to my cousin's felt amazing. It was also interesting how bad the Las Vegas trip went and how he gambled and lost all of our money and it was cool that when I went on the casino boat and gambled, I walked away with money.

I started worrying about money and how I was going to pay for everything, but my husband kept paying for everything. One day, someone I bowled with had to butcher a cow, and they had all this extra beef and no freezer space for it, so they offered it to me. I got to see God's miracles happening by constantly blessing me and my kids in meeting our needs. I found myself talking to Jesus and praying and reading my Bible a lot. I had prayed that I was willing to give my husband up if that is what it took to stop her from destroying any more marriages. I begged God to help me find someone who would love me and that I would not have to spend my life alone. I remember specifically doing this on the back deck and reading in the Bible that I will have sons and they will walk me down the aisle and I would be filled with joy. I was led directly to the Bible verse (Isaiah 62:5). "For as a young man marries a virgin, So shall your sons marry you; And as the bridegroom rejoices over the bride, so shall your God rejoice over you." (Isaiah 62:5). The Lord answered me and told me I will marry and that I will have sons marry me. Also, that my groom and the Lord would be filled with joy over me.

At this time, my husband came to the house to get something and saw me reading the Bible out back and made fun of me, saying, "So you are doing your Bible banging thing are you?" I only felt very, very sorry for him. When he left, I wasn't as upset that he was making fun of me as I was that he was disrespecting the Lord. I kept saying over and over how sorry I was to the Lord that he did that to Him. Jesus was my best friend, and this really hurt me. I realized that my husband was such a fool. He just didn't get it at all.

When I read the Bible, and it said I would have sons marry me. I couldn't see how that could be possible though because I only had one son. This was around the time that God spoke to me, through His word, and then so many more times to follow throughout my life. I had been faithful at attending church and taking the kids with me almost every Sunday by myself. I read the Bible stories to the kids and sang the songs from the Sunday school days to my kids at bath time. I taught them to pray and we did this every day. I was very consistent with this with them. This is something I will never regret doing with my children. I worked very hard to instill the Lord in my children.

One of the days my husband was there, we were in the garage, and I said to my husband, "You are going to try and take the kids away from me, aren't you?"

His reply was, "No, I don't want them." I asked if there was any chance of him coming back, and his answer was, "No. I don't love you and I can't love you and I don't want to love you ever again."

I said, "I just needed to know because there were a few guys interested in going out with me and I thought about going out with them but I wanted to make sure we are through first." His comment was that no man could ever love me or want me and that I was making all of that up to try and make him jealous. How very wrong he was. I did have four different men that wanted to go out with me. This was the closure for me. I went back into the house. I took our wedding pictures off the walls and I took my wedding ring off. Once I made that decision, there was no turning back. When my mind was made up, it was final. We were done.

One of the four guys interested in me was a bachelor that lived in the same town. I wasn't really interested in him. Another guy I met by a couple I knew through bowling tried setting us up and had dinner for us to meet. That didn't work out. Then there was this guy who went to the adjoining church I attended, and people were working to try and have us meet but that never happened.

I hadn't worked for a long time outside the house because I was a stay-at-home mom. I had worked in the office, but my degree didn't amount to anything anymore because word processing didn't even exist anymore and that was what my degree was in. I signed up for a temporary agency to work in the office. I tried to figure out where to go now with my life. I knew I would have to go to work to take care of my kids.

Another thing that also weighed heavy on my mind and was one of my big concerns, "Do I have AIDS?" I made an appointment with my doctor and I asked him if he could run the test for me. He asked me what was going on. I explained everything while crying. He was so nice to me and gave me a big hug. He said how very sorry he was and that I had nothing to worry about since he was going to take care of me by running every sexually transmitted disease out there to make sure I was okay. He told me that the AIDS test had to be ran twice, once again in another six months just to be sure. He ran all the tests, and thank God, I didn't have any sexual transmitted disease. I just kept thinking, so help me God, if my husband gives me AIDS because of him messing around with the woman who has been with almost every man at work, I will kill him. I swear. Thank God both of my tests came back negative.

I remember driving around another town in our county that I never lived in and thinking to myself, "How wonderful it would be to be able to live there and get away from the town I was in." I didn't know what life had in store for me next, but I knew the Lord would catch it all.

About the Author

Rose Marie Arthur grew up extremely fast, taking on huge responsibilities at a young age for most of her life. These responsibilities led her to working with people young and old and in-between with all sorts of disabilities. She served on the board for MR/DD for years. She is a mother of four children. For people who know her, Rose Marie Arthur is her pen name and it is very special to her. As a Christian all her life, she has experienced many God moments, and she shares them in her books, *One Thing after Another* and its sequel, *One Thing after Another and Another*. As an author, she hopes to help people through their darkest times and inspire people to follow Christ. She lives with her husband and family in the Chicagoland Area.

CONTEMPORARY WRITERS IN CHRISTIAN PERSPECTIVE
EDITED BY RODERICK JELLEMA

Graham Greene

A CRITICAL ESSAY
BY MARTIN TURNELL

WILLIAM B. EERDMANS/PUBLISHER

CONTENTS

3

Introductory

GRAHAM GREENE HAS DIVIDED HIS FICTION INTO TWO GROUPS: novels and "entertainments." His aim is evidently to draw a distinction between his serious work and the lighter fare, the adventure stories or "thrillers." A few of his critics have remarked on the similarity between the works of the two groups, but they have not explored the implications. It is difficult not to feel a little doubtful about the validity of the distinction. A writer may try his hand at different forms, but the man behind them all is the same person. The genuine writer cannot cut himself entirely in two, turning on or shutting off his deepest interests and preoccupations at will, or take time off from his study of the human condition in order to provide his audience with light reading.

When we look more closely at the works in the two groups, we find in fact that there are a number of basic similarities, that the differences are much more a matter of angle or emphasis than either form or material. The central figures in the best of the novels from *The Man Within* to *A Burnt-out Case,* and in the "entertainments" from *Stamboul Train* to *The Ministry of Fear,* is the "hunted man": the man who is literally on the run like Andrews in *The Man Within,* the "whisky priest" in *The Power and the Glory* or Raven in *A Gun for Sale,* or characters like Scobie in *The Heart of the Matter* or Querry in *A Burnt-out Case* who are seeking escape from some inner weakness and the psychological situation it has created. The resemblances do not end there. Among the most distinctive characteristics of the typical Greene character are an unhappy childhood, a domineering, usually a violent father, and an ambivalent attitude towards a minor public school. The unhappy childhood and the domineering father are decisive in the case of Andrews, Raven and of Anthony Farrant in *England Made Me*:

> He remembered his father at home, domineering, brutal, a conscious master, not chary of his blows to either child or wife . . . (*The Man Within*).

5

Anthony learning (the beating in the nursery, the tears before boarding school) to keep a stiff upper lip, Anthony learning (the beating in the study when he brought home the smutty book with the pretty pictures) that you must honour other men's sisters ... yes, he loved Anthony and he ruined Anthony and he was tormented by Anthony until the end. The telegrams, the telephoned messages, the face grinning over the bed-rail: 'I've resigned' (*England Made Me*).

Raven, too, was the son of a man of violence. His father was hanged for murder; his mother committed suicide; he was sent to an "institution" and eventually became a paid murderer:

'I've dreamed I opened a door, a kitchen door, and there was my mother — she'd cut her throat — she looked ugly — her head nearly off — she'd sawn at it — with a bread knife. . . .'

'And after that, there was a Home ... I got beaten a lot at the start, solitary confinement, bread and water, all the rest of the homy stuff' (*A Gun for Sale*).

In all these cases the central character is seen to be a product of environment. Whatever the social level, whether it is genteel as in *England Made Me* or proletarian as in *A Gun for Sale,* the weaknesses of the central characters are the outcome of a decaying social system. The main characters in *England Made Me,* as well as most of the minor characters, have betrayed everything they once stood for and are reduced to a group of "exiles" and "outsiders" gyrating in a "wilderness of [their] own contriving." We are told of Kate Farrant, the woman with an incestuous inclination for her wastrel brother:

In the last resort she hadn't the energy to be completely ruthless. Good Looks and Conscience, she thought, the fine flowers of our class. We're done, we're broke, we belong to the past, we haven't the character or the energy to do more than hang on to something new for whatever we can make out of it.

It is perhaps the sense that he is depicting a society which has lost its nerve which accounts in part for another of Graham Greene's most pronounced characteristics. "It had been a massacre on the Elizabethan scale," we read in one of the closing scenes in *The Ministry of Fear.* What we find in the works of both groups is an atmosphere of violence and extremes: an atmosphere in which the misfit turns into the rebel and the fugitive; the misfit who is a danger to a disintegrating society,

6

but who is nevertheless, even when he is a murderer like Raven, somehow superior to it and becomes its victim.

I have suggested that the writer behind all the books is the same person. It follows from this that they provide an expression or, better, an outlet, for something in his personal make-up. This explains a number of things: the resemblance of some of the early novels to traditional adventure stories, the intrusion into the "entertainments" of some of the themes from the novels and — more important than either — the attempt to combine the two forms in the later novels which produces what a friendly critic has described as "spiritual melodrama." It also explains the highly accomplished craftsmanship which is common to both forms: the narrative gift, the slickness in the presentation of the story, the cinematic "cutting," the skill with which the writer uses the "point of view," and a journalistic flair for the vivid detail.

This is the opening of *A Gun for Sale*:

> Murder didn't mean much to Raven. It was just a new job. You had to be careful. You had to use your brains. It was not a question of hatred. He had only seen the Minister once: he had been pointed out to Raven as he walked down the new housing estate between the little lit Christmas trees, an old, rather grubby man without any friends, who was said to love humanity.

In six lines the scene is set: a gunman has been hired to assassinate the minister of some foreign state. The murderer, with his terrible background, is deficient in human feeling; he has no hatred for his victim; it is just a "new job." Later in the book Christmas trees and decorations will turn up again as symbols of the precarious stability, or outer stability, of the dying society in which Raven is a misfit.

This is a glimpse of the Red Militia in Mexico: the men who are in pursuit of the "whisky priest," who in the end catch and shoot him:

> The squad of police made their way back to the station: they walked raggedly with rifles slung anyhow: ends of cotton where buttons should have been: a puttee slipping down over the ankle: small men with black secret Indian eyes.

The scene is presented with remarkable economy. The author has an unerring eye for the vivid detail: the slovenly turnout,

7

the missing buttons, the slipping puttee, the crafty "secret" eyes. The laconic prose with its skilful use of colons reproduces the straggling gait of the marchers. The new order is no better than the old. The sloppiness and scruffiness of its representatives are a reflection of its lack of civilized values, its emptiness, its vacancy.

The Making of a Novelist

"IT WAS JUST BECAUSE THE VISIBLE UNIVERSE WHICH HE WAS careful to treat with the highest kind of justice was determined for him at an early age," Greene wrote in a remarkable essay on Henry James in *The Lost Childhood,* "that his family background is of such interest."

There is little doubt that Greene's own early years were at least as important for his future development as they were for Henry James. He was born in 1904, educated at one of the smaller public schools where his father was headmaster, and at Oxford. He rebelled against the conditions of school life, ran away and was sent to a psychoanalyst for treatment. This is how he describes it in the terrifying essay in *The Lost Childhood* called "The Revolver in the Corner Cupboard":

> I emerged from those delightful months in London spent at my analyst's house — perhaps the happiest months of my life — correctly orientated, able to take a proper extrovert interest in my fellows (the jargon rises to the lips), but wrung dry.

The treatment did, indeed, have what are now known as "side effects." They were "boredom" and "aridity." In earlier years there had been several semi-serious attempts at suicide: drinking "hypo"; eating deadly nightshade; swallowing a large quantity of aspirin before a swim in the deserted school baths. Now, he says, "I had stumbled on the perfect cure" for boredom. The "perfect cure" was the game with the revolver which gives the essay its title. What he did was to load one chamber of a tiny revolver found in a "corner cupboard," spin the drum and then

8

I put the muzzle of the revolver in my right ear and pulled the trigger. There was a minute click, and looking down at the chamber, I could see that the charge had moved into place. I was out by one.

There are some revealing glimpses of school life and the early years in *The Lawless Roads* and *Journey without Maps*:

> . . . one was aware of fear and hate, a kind of lawlessness — appalling cruelties could be practiced without a second thought; one met for the first time characters, adult and adolescent, who bore about them the genuine quality of evil. There was Collifax, who practiced torments with dividers; Mr. Cranden with three grim chins, a dusty gown, a kind of demoniac sensuality; from these heights evil declined towards Parlow, whose desk was filled with minute photographs — advertisements for art photos. Hell lay about them in their infancy (*The Lawless Roads*).

It was the sense of evil that led to faith:

> And so 'faith came to one — shapelessly, without dogma, a presence above a croquet lawn, something associated with violence, cruelty, evil across the way. One began to believe in heaven because one believed in hell . . . but for a while it was only hell one could picture with a certain intimacy — the pitchpine partitions of dormitories where everybody was never quiet at the same time; lavatories without locks . . . (*ibid.*).

Greene tells us somewhere that he had always suffered from nightmares. They play a considerable part in the novels. This is a description of one of his own dreams:

> It was only many years later that Evil came into my dreams: the man with gold teeth and rubber surgical gloves; the old woman with ringworm; the man with his throat cut dragging himself across the carpet to the bed (*Journey without Maps*).

When he left Balliol he took up journalism and worked for a time on a provincial newspaper at Nottingham where, in 1926, he became a Catholic:

> There seemed to be a seediness about the place you couldn't get to the same extent elsewhere, and seediness has a very deep appeal: even the seediness of civilisation, the "tarts" in Bond Street, the smell of cooking greens off Tottenham Court Road, the little tight-waisted Jews in the Strand. It seems to satisfy, temporarily, the sense of nostalgia for something lost; it seems to represent a stage further back (*ibid.*).

9

Another glimpse of Nottingham:

> The municipal "tart" paced up and down by the largest cinema, old and haggard and unused. Her trade was spoilt; there were too many girls who hadn't a proper sense of values, who would give you a good time in return for a fish tea (*ibid.*).

These fragments of autobiography throw considerable light on Greene's sources and on the conception of life that we find in his fiction: the rebel against convention and respectability who becomes the "hunted" schoolboy; an abnormal streak which prompts an adolescent to gamble with his life as Scobie will gamble with his soul; the association of religion with violence and cruelty and evil; a taste for "seediness" which will produce the admirable account of Brighton in *Brighton Rock* and of the provincial setting in *A Gun for Sale* as well as a trait which is much less admirable: a tone that varies from astringency to sourness, the sourness evident in the gratuitously cruel picture of the municipal harlot, "old and haggard and unused."

There is also something which artistically is more important than any of these traits. "If ever a man's imagination was clouded by the Pit, it was James's," Greene wrote in the essay from which I have already quoted. There is a marked contrast in the presentation of evil by the two novelists. In James it is felt to be the sign of a mature view of life; in Greene, I do not have this feeling. James's evil is a powerful, diabolical force which leaves no room for complacency. Greene's evil is something which belongs to childhood and adolescence: it is associated with the school bully, the sadistic or perverted schoolmaster, and a figure which might have come from a "horror comic" or a horror film: "the man with gold teeth and rubber surgical gloves." The absence from the novels of any compelling apprehension of evil in the Jamesian sense, or the presence of an evil which is symbolized, significantly, by the juvenile delinquent and the "spiv" explains our feeling that the novels somehow lack the mature approach to experience that we find in the great writer.

The Early Novels

SOME OF THE PRINCIPAL CHARACTERISTICS OF WHAT WAS TO
become the Greene hero are apparent in Andrews, the protagonist of his first novel:

> Andrews's character was built of superficial dreams, sentimentali-
> ty, cowardice, and yet he was constantly made aware beneath all
> these of an uncomfortable questioning critic. So now this other
> inhabitant of his body wondered whether he had not mistaken
> peace for inhumanity. Peace was not cowardly nor sentimental
> nor filled with illusion. Peace was a sanity which he did not
> believe he had ever known.

Andrews is the smuggler's son: the son of the violent, domineering father who has been blighted in childhood and who
betrays the gang by turning king's evidence, but whose cow-
ardice is also responsible for the death of the infinitely superior
woman whom he was to have married. The essential characteristics of many future Greene heroes are there: "superficial dreams," "cowardice," "sentimentality." The "superficial
dreams" are the gap between the character and reality, one of
the causes of his failure to fit in because they prevent a proper
appreciation of the issues at stake and of his own motives with
the result that they foster illusion. "Cowardice" and "sentimentality" are inseparable: the deadly combination which is responsible for every kind of betrayal. Andrews's weakness has led to
the betrayal of his accomplices and to the death of his girl. The
novel closes with his confession to a murder that he did not
commit and to his arrest. But there is a secular-psychological
"redemption":

> Andrews did not look back upon the cottage. Regret had gone,
> even remembrance of the graceless body abandoned there. To his
> own surprise he felt happy and at peace, for his father was slain
> and yet a self remained, a self which knew neither lust, blasphe-
> my nor cowardice, but only peace and curiosity for the dark
> which deepened around him. You were always right, he said, in
> the hope, not yet belief, that there was something in the night
> which would hear him, the fourth time it brought peace. His

11

father's ghost had been a stubborn ghost, but it was laid at last, and he need no longer be torn in two between that spirit and the stern unresting critic which was wont to speak. I am that critic, he said with a sense of discovery and exhilaration.

The reference to "the stern unresting critic" looks back to another important phrase in the earlier passage on Andrews's character:

He was constantly made aware beneath all these of an uncomfortable questioning critic.

The words suggest a strength, an insight into his own motives which are not in fact there. It is the illusion of strength on the part of the weak man which fosters his weaknesses and produces the moral confusion that is particularly characteristic of the protagonists of the Christian novels. What we also notice even in this early work is that there is something suspect about the prose: another kind of sentimentality hiding a still deeper weakness. In order to establish the existence of "the stern unresting critic," the novelist uses some questionable romantic clichés: the emotive words, "peace," "darkness," "hope, not yet belief," the "ghost" that is laid, the fanciful metamorphosis of the coward into a "new man."

Although the action in this first novel is seen exclusively from the point of view of the protagonist, he remains a fluid, amorphous, indeterminate figure. The minor characters, too, are shadowy and appear to have been borrowed largely from R. L. Stevenson whose influence on the book is heavy. The background is as shadowy and indeterminate as the characters. We are not told the period in which the story takes place: we are left to infer that the author is describing a smuggling incident in the early part of the nineteenth century. Greene's development in the novels that followed is apparent in a number of ways: the greater subtlety and complexity of the protagonists; the skill displayed in the delineation of environment and the multiplication of the "points of view" which helps to weld the novels into a whole and gives their structure its firmness and clarity.

Whatever its artistic limitations, there are two factors of great importance in Greene's first novel. The first is very clearly indicated by the title. The real theme is the contrast between the "inner" and the "outer" man. Outwardly Andrews is a mess: a mixture of "superficial dreams," "sentimentality" and "cow-ardice." But the real man — "the man within" — is "the stern unresting critic." I am not convinced, as I have already said, by the metamorphosis or, better, the emergence of the "new man," and the triumphant cry with which the identification of the real Andrews with "the stern unresting critic" is announced sounds to me hollow. Yet the theme is central in Greene's fiction and is developed with greater insight and subtlety in the later novels from *The Power and the Glory* to *The Comedians.* In *The Power and the Glory* the priest who soaks up the whisky and fornicates is outwardly a mess, but the real man is the martyr who emerges when he faces the firing squad. For here there is "conversion" in the sense of a deepening of religious feeling in the man who is already a believer which is much more impres-sive than the secular "conversion" which ends with suicide in the first novel. In *The Heart of the Matter* the process is reversed. Outwardly Scobie is a model man: upright, respected, a practicing Christian. In this case, however, it is the inner man who is rotten: the sentimentalist who is guilty of sacrilegious communion, adultery and finally suicide because he cannot face the effect of his successive betrayals on his wife or his mistress.

The other factor of great importance in Greene's first novel is the band or gang or smugglers. It is scarcely too much to say that in the books which followed this one "parties," "gangs," "bands," "rings" — particularly spy rings — and "groups" become the hub round which the entire action revolves.

The Name of Action, Greene's second novel, is a sort of Ruritanian fantasy about a rich young man going to a foreign country where he finances and joins in a conspiracy to remove the local dictator whose wife, being a Graham Greene charac-ter, he naturally seduces. It is not a good novel and the author has been adamant in refusing to allow it to be reprinted or included in his collected works, but in some respects it is an advance on *The Man Within.* The group of conspirators plays a much more dynamic role; the setting — the picture of a country living under dictatorship — is more firmly drawn, and the minor characters are more sharply individualized than the smugglers in the first novel.

Writers on Greene have commented on the part played in his

work by topical events. *The Name of Action* was the first of several books dealing, directly or indirectly, with dictatorship and revolution. *England Made Me* was suggested by an international financial swindle; *The Power and the Glory* by the religious persecution in Mexico; *The Ministry of Fear* by the second world war; and other books like *Brighton Rock, Stamboul Train* and *The Confidential Agent* by the gangsterism, spying and political assassinations which have become the commonplaces of life in the twentieth century.

The topical setting has obvious practical advantages. The situation suggests the landscape and the figures, enabling the novelist to establish his characters with the minimum of trouble. For in each of his books he is provided with a group which is a part of the setting and almost ready-made: the smugglers in *The Man Within*; the financiers and expatriates in *England Made Me;* the travellers in *Stamboul Train;* the "spivs" and juvenile delinquents in *Brighton Rock;* police, peasants and expatriates in *The Power and the Glory;* civil servants, police and natives in *The Heart of the Matter*; the missionaries, lepers and expatriates in *A Burnt-out Case.*

This explains the position of the protagonist. The novels deal with the protagonist's contacts with the group. He may be attached to a group, the prisoner of a group or a fugitive from it, but in every instance the effect is twofold. It sets up a movement of opposition and contagion. When he is not actually a fugitive, the protagonist feels that he is a misfit, an outsider who does not really belong, but at the same time his contacts with it foster his weaknesses, provide the temptations which eventually bring him down.

The pattern is clearest in the Catholic novels. The Catholic — the wayward Catholic, or the bad Catholic or the lapsed Catholic — is at the center. He is surrounded by minor characters who represent various degrees of belief, unbelief or disbelief, as they represent various degrees of corruption. They are largely stock figures, stereotypes who in slightly different guises turn up in different books: the man from the small public school trying to live it down in *England Made Me* and *The Heart of the Matter;* the Fellows, who though not Catholics are a preliminary sketch for the Scobies, and the "churchy" mother, always reading from the lives of the saints, in *The Power and*

14

the Glory; Rycker, the miserable *rat de bénitier* with his "babydoll" wife in *A Burnt-out Case;* the racketeer in *Brighton Rock* and still more Ida Arnold, who is something of a caricature: the product of a secularized lower-middle class who believes only in the antics of the planchette, good-naturedly opens her legs to all comers, but "knows the difference between Right and Wrong."

Religion and Sex: the Importance of Brighton Rock

IT IS INTERESTING TO WATCH THE GROWTH OF THE RELIGIOUS element in the novels. It appears for the first time in the person of a minor character in *England Made Me*. Minty is the public school boy, the failure, the remittance man eking out a living as a small-time journalist in Sweden. He is honest, decent, chaste — he is horribly embarrassed at having to lend his room to Anthony Farrant so that he can fornicate with his girl friend — the victim, as surely as the wastrel whom he obliges, of environment: a product of the decay of the genteel tradition.

The presence of one minor character who is a practicing Christian is not sufficient to change the novelist's approach to his material. It is not until *Brighton Rock* that we meet protagonists who are, or rather who were brought up as Catholics. They are the delinquent youth and the waitress who marry in a register office, who have just enough conscience to know that they have done wrong, and just enough intelligence to realize that whatever their shortcomings they are different from their fellows. This may not appear much, but it is the sign of a major change in the novelist's approach.

Although Greene enjoyed his first popular success with *Stamboul Train,* which was also the first of the "entertainments," it was *Brighton Rock* that established his reputation as one of the leading English novelists of his age. It is a highly accomplished piece of work which in spite of its horrifying ending deserved its success. It is a good deal more besides. It is of particular

15

importance for a full understanding of Greene's novels and of his later development.

Brighton Rock is still described on the title page as an "entertainment," and in the lists of the author's books at the beginning of each volume of the library editions as a "novel." This classification looks odd, but there is a reason for it. Greene's conception of the adventure story and his use of the "thriller" technique owe a great deal to an illustrious model. In *The Secret Agent,* perhaps his greatest novel, Joseph Conrad adapted the form of the "thriller" to serious material and produced an indubitable masterpiece. The book is a masterpiece because there is perfect fusion of form and matter and because of the originality of the enterprise. Dostoevsky had done something of the sort in *Crime and Punishment,* but so far as I can recall it was the first time that it had been attempted in English.

Although Greene has preserved the distinction between "novels" and "entertainments," and has written several books since *Brighton Rock* which carry this label, we can see that in *Brighton Rock* he deliberately attempted for the first time to combine the two forms and to write a book of the same kind as *The Secret Agent.* I do not think that in *Brighton Rock* the fusion is complete; I think that it stands alone in his work as an impressive hybrid: an "entertainment-novel." What is beyond doubt is that it not only prepared the way for *The Power and the Glory,* but made that novel possible.

It might be argued that even in *Brighton Rock* religion is incidental, that with two such shabby and wayward protagonists the contrast between believers and unbelievers is too faint to be really effective. This view seems to me to overlook a much subtler, a much more fundamental change. In all the novels which preceded it, the decaying social system and its corrosive effect on the characters are described in purely secular terms. In *Brighton Rock* the world of gangsters, juvenile delinquents and "spivs" is no longer merely the world of gangsters, juvenile delinquents and "spivs": it is identifiable for the first time with what has been called "the fallen world." The characters are not simply misfits or outsiders or even criminals: they are felt to be *sinners.* A new dimension has been added to Greene's fiction.

It is now possible to see a pattern emerging, or what the French call, a trifle pompously, the *sujet profond.* Greene's subject, like that of any genuinely serious novelist, is the human condition: the fate of man in a world in which the consequences of original sin are rampant, and the redemption of the sinner through suffering. For the purely secular approach of the earlier novels has gone. He is no longer concerned with mere social decay in a religionless world; the disasters are the results of sin and must be atoned for by suffering. Once this has been said, the other characteristics to which I have drawn attention — the topicality which gives many of the books their immediate appeal, the "groups," "parties," "gangs," "bands" and "rings," — fall into place. They stand for and are part of the contemporary world. In this way the "new dimension" brings what might be called a dual environment: the contemporary world is very much with us, but it is seen against the background of eternity.

In the course of this essay I shall have a number of serious reservations to make about the *quality* of the religion in Greene's novels and its responsibility for what I am bound to consider artistic failings. It is therefore right for me to say now that I regard him as an important and very distinguished writer and that the presence of religion in his work gives him something which is inevitably lacking in the purely secularist writer — a point which will receive further discussion in my final chapter.

Religion gives the novels that other dimension which is not to be found in the secularist writer, but from the time of its first real appearance in *Brighton Rock* it is not something which imposes itself on a society or a group: if it is not precisely a product of modern conditions, it is a religion that is undoubtedly deeply colored and to a considerable degree determined by them. The kind of religion that we find in *The Power and the Glory, The Heart of the Matter* and *A Burnt-out Case* is seen in the first place as a highly emotional charge, creating an atmosphere in which theological problems, or rather moral-theological problems, are bandied about, in which religious standards are constantly evoked only to show how very far short of them the behavior of the protagonist falls, in which familiar dogmas are given a new and sometimes highly discon-

17

certing look as when, for example, redemption appears to involve, or to be confused with, a Catholic suicide.

It follows that far from being the world of humdrum, conventional religion, the world of Graham Greene is the world of a highly idiosyncratic religion. His aim in the main religious novels is apparently to take us behind the scenes, to discover special virtues in people whose conduct is invariably at odds with their profession. In this way he gives the impression that it is somehow the idiosyncratic, the personal, the morally unorthodox, which is pleasing to God. His religion is very much the religion of the fallen world, but the fact that religion is religion gives the novels their supercharged atmosphere.

"This Congo is a region of the mind," said Greene in the dedicatory letter at the beginning of *A Burnt-out Case*. The setting of the novels matches the quality of the religion and contributes to the unity of the best of them. The Mexico of *The Power and the Glory* and the Gold Coast of *The Heart of the Matter* are as much a "region of the mind" as the Congo of *A Burnt-out Case*. It is a grim, depressing, suffocating region, but though it is dead and deadening, a region that drains all hope from life, it is still a region which appears somehow to provoke terrifying events.

What I want to suggest next is that the lurid atmosphere in which whisky priests and Scobies move and have their being has had the effect of misleading some of Greene's critics, diverting them from their proper task, which is the scrutiny of the writer's text, and encouraging them instead to discuss general theological problems: to speculate on the ways of God to man. In a review of *A Burnt-out Case* in *Ramparts,* for example, we find the reviewer speculating about the protagonist's chances of salvation as earlier writers on Greene had speculated about Scobie's: fairly evenly divided between those who thought him damned and those who almost saw in the suicide a new kind of saint.

> A critical method [wrote the reviewer in *Ramparts,* Vol. I, No. 1, May 1962, p. 86] which limits itself to examination of style, psychology, character, naturalism and the like will overlook the most central aspect of Greene's work: man as a metaphysical being.

This is the reverse of the thesis that I am going to defend here. What I shall argue is that there is something wrong with the quality of the religion in Greene's novels and that this is reflected in his use of language. That a critic should be able to brush aside "style, psychology, character, naturalism and the like" as more or less unimportant is striking evidence of the way in which Greene has succeeded by the peculiar atmosphere which his fiction generates in putting his critics off the scent, leading them away from the place where their enquiry should start: his prose style.

The critic whom I have just quoted praises *A Burnt-out Case* because in it he finds "none of the flashy sentences and trite figures of speech which abound in his earlier works." This praise, as we shall see later, is well deserved: the mistake lies in treating "the flashy sentences and trite figures of speech" as though they are no more than blemishes in novels treating importantly with "man as a metaphysical being," in the assumption that the great theme is somehow independent of the language in which it is expressed and transcends mere words. The only answer we can make is that if great themes are treated in a language which is "flashy" or "trite," we shall almost certainly discover that there is something wrong with the treatment.

In Greene's first novel we find this sentence:

> The blackberry twigs plucked at him and tried to hold him with small endearments, twisted small thorns into his clothes with a restraint like a caress, *as though they were the fingers of a harlot in a crowded bar.*

The italics in the quotation are mine. I think that the *Ramparts* critic would probably describe the words as "flashy": to me they are something more and something different. This is a typical Greene image which occurs not merely in his first novel, but in nearly all the novels of his maturity. It is of the essence of these images that they call attention to themselves. They seem to do so by trying to establish what Aristotle, in his definition of metaphor, called the perception of similarity in dissimilars. The comparison between the thorns catching the fugitive's clothing and the harlot fingering his flies in a crowded bar is plainly too farfetched to be a success. The words are not dictated by the subject; they are put in from outside and

19

resemble the conceits used by the lesser poets of the seventeenth century rather than the dynamic conceit of a Donne or a Marvell where there is a genuine perception of similarity in dissimilars. In short, the image reveals already Greene's tendency to operate by overstatement, to introduce a dash of sensationalism into the commonplace, to heighten ordinary experience. What is also characteristic is the way in which the author draws on the sexual connection for this type of image. These are other examples:

> The school and he were joined by a painful reluctant coition, a passionless coition that leaves everything to regret, nothing to love, everything to hate, but cannot destroy the idea: we are one body (*England Made Me*).

> He saw a girl in a dirty shift spread out on the packing cases like a fish on a counter (*The Heart of the Matter*).

> The dangerous desire to confide grew in Father Thomas's mind like the pressure of an orgasm (*A Burnt-out Case*).

I have on occasion been taken to task by Greene's admirers for adopting what appears to them to be a slightly puritanical attitude towards his treatment of sexuality. This is a complete misunderstanding. I probably enjoy his salacious jokes a good deal more than many of his admirers. My criticisms are based on purely artistic grounds. I am trying to show that the use of a certain type of image reveals a defective attitude towards sexuality, as I shall try to show later that a not dissimilar use of religious imagery reveals defects in the novelist's conception of religion. The recurrence of the sexual image in book after book, in the least appropriate contexts, surely suggests that there is something obsessive, something unbalanced, about the writer's preoccupation with sexuality. The image of the girl in the dirty shift "spread out on the packing cases like a fish on a counter" reinforces the impression created by the first example: that the sexual connection is somehow furtive, dirty, degrading. And what could be more forced than the comparison between a priest's desire to discuss his religious doubts and "the pressure of an orgasm"? It is a curious fact that though Greene's novels abound in incidents of fornication and adultery, I cannot remember a single instance of a really satisfactory connection even in the "entertainments." It is either an act dripping with guilt or a quick wiggle which is over in a matter of seconds:

> She only regretted the promptitude of the embrace. . . . He was with her, he was in her, he was away from her, brushing his hair, whistling a tune (*It's a Battlefield*).

The obsessiveness becomes much more pronounced in the religious novels. These are samples from *Brighton Rock*:

> He lay still thinking: "What a dream!" and then heard the stealthy movement of his parents in the other bed. It was Saturday night. His father panted like a man at the end of a race and his mother made a horrifying sound of pleasurable pain.

> You could know everything there was in the world and yet if you were ignorant of that one dirty scramble you knew nothing.

> Phil opened one eye — yellow with sexual effort — and watched apprehensively.

In still another passage Pinkie broods over

> the frightening weekly exercise of his parents which he watched from his single bed.

Graham Greene once reproached the present writer for saying of the last two quotations that they showed an abnormal attitude towards human nature. He is well known to be a warm admirer of the late Percy Lubbock's *The Craft of Fiction* with its emphasis on the novelist's "point of view." He argued that in *Brighton Rock* you have to allow for the writer's "point of view," that the emphasis on the "single" bed and the odd use of the adjective "yellow" could not be interpreted as a reflection of his own attitude because in this book he was depicting an abnormal character. I was not convinced by this argument in so far as it applies to Greene's own novels. A novelist must obviously be free to introduce what are known as "abnormal" characters into his fiction and great novelists have often done so. What matters is the way in which they are presented. Equally, all imaginative writers put something of themselves into their characters, but once again it is a matter of degree. What happens in *Brighton Rock* is that the degree of identification between novelist and character is excessive and at times disturbs the balance of the book. The reference to the "single" bed and the comments on the "dirty scramble" are not the comments of an adolescent, abnormal or otherwise: they are the comments of the author. In other words, the character is used as an instrument for the projection of certain highly personal preoccupations of the novelist. I must therefore agree with the acute observation by the authors of a laudatory study of Greene who speak of "the fear of the body evident from the beginning in Greene's fiction and strongest in *Brighton Rock*" (K. Allott & M. Farris: *The Art of Graham Greene,* pp. 236-7).

The Power and the Glory

The Power and the Glory IS THE MOST POPULAR OF GREENE'S novels. The reasons are plain. The theme of the persecution of religion by the police state is more than topical: it is one of the great dilemmas of our time and marks the merging of the topical into the universal. There is a blend, too, of what seems best in the novels and the "entertainments." The "hunted man" appears to be a valid symbol of the problems of the age. The distinction between the priest's office and the human failings of the holder provides the novelist with a perfect opportunity of demonstrating his thesis on the difference between the "inner" and the "outer" man, between conventional Catholicism and the behind-the-scenes Catholicism. It is because the formal division between the priest and the man corresponds to a division in the author's own personality that it is a curiously suitable vehicle for his talents, for the diffusion of that highly charged atmosphere which is regarded as pre-eminently Greene's.

The contrast between the office and its holder is glaring. The priest chose the priesthood, on his own showing, out of vanity. He was the son of humble parents who wanted to "get on" and a vocation for the priesthood was the obvious way. When the persecution breaks out he becomes a drinker, a "whisky priest." Without any genuine love or passion he seduces an Indian woman when visiting her village to administer the sacraments, and there is a child. Yet he is superior to Padre José, the priest who conformed to the state decrees, abandoned his calling and married. And because he is so, the "whisky priest" becomes a

22

martyr. The title underlines, and seems intended to underline, the novelist's thesis. Those who appear holy in the eyes of the world are something far different in God's eyes: it is the sinner — almost the public sinner — the man riddled with every human weakness except one who is the real saint.

Technically, the novel is a considerable advance on any of its predecessors and its range is a good deal wider. There is a systematic attempt to present the different kinds and degrees of belief or unbelief, to show how they harmonize or conflict, reinforce or qualify one another. The unshakable belief of the priest is matched with the unshakable disbelief of the communist lieutenant, or what he takes for unshakable disbelief:

> He was a mystic, too, and what he had experienced was vacancy — a complete certainty in the existence of a dying, cooling world, of human beings who had evolved for no purpose at all.

Yet he remains somehow unsure of himself, mysteriously attracted to the priest whom he is to execute, even trying unsuccessfully to persuade the laicized Padre José to hear his confession before the execution. There is a similar contrast in the people behind them: the childlike faith of the frightened downtrodden Indians and the hopeless resignation of the urban crowds who have been "cured of superstition" and have nothing better to do than mill aimlessly around the streets until the curfew sends them slinking home. There are other individual contrasts: the priest and the cowardly Padre José who refuses the unbelieving lieutenant's invitation to shrive the "whisky priest" before he is shot; the unreal piety of the "churchy" women; the Lutherans who "don't hold with the Mass"; the unbelieving bandit who tries to save the priest; Mr. Tench and the Fellows, expatriates who have no religion and whose world has crumbled.

The role of children in the novel is particularly striking: the priest's illegitimate daughter who is already corrupted by the world and spiritually doomed; the unbelieving daughter of the Fellows who was moving towards the priest or the faith he stands for when she met with a violent end. Most curious of all is the chorus of native children unimpressed by the communist militia and mocking Padre José when his wife calls him, impatiently, to bed.

23

The contrasts are driven home by the multiplication of the "points of view." Most of the action is seen through the eyes of the priest, but we also have the points of view of the lieutenant, Padre José, Mr. Tench, the Fellows. What this adds up to is a firm, clear structure, the appearance of strength and solidity, the suggestion of depth.

If we applied the standard proposed by the *Ramparts* critic, if we gave the highest marks to the novelist who treats man as a "metaphysical being," we should evidently have to award very high marks to *The Power and the Glory*. Yet when we study the text more closely doubts arise; we have the impression that there is a gap between the superstructure and the materials out of which it is built — the language. The sensational images which had made sporadic appearances in the earlier novels come streaming from the novelist's pen:

> The man's dark suit and sloping shoulders reminded Mr. Tench uncomfortably of a coffin, and death was in his carious mouth already.

> He followed her meekly, tripping in the long peon's trousers with the happiness wiped off his face like the survivor of a wreck.

> A few men moved in the hammocks — a large unshaven jaw hung over the side like something left unsold on a butcher's counter. . . .

The comparison between the priest's sloping shoulders and a coffin points, crudely, to his end. There is exaggeration in the comparison between the vanished happiness and a "survivor of a wreck," which seems to be a reference to the state of the Church of Mexico. We get a shock when an unshaven jaw is compared to "something left unsold on a butcher's counter." The image is applied to one of the communist policemen and expresses, melodramatically, not merely disapproval of the scruffy communists, but what I have called the author's sour attitude towards the human race.

I want to turn now to a longer passage which describes the priest's unspoken thoughts on his way back to the village where he had seduced the Indian peasant:

> In any case, even if he could have gone south and avoided the village, it was only one more surrender: the years behind him were littered with similar surrenders — the feast days and the fast days and days of abstinence had been the first to go: then he had ceased to trouble more than occasionally about his breviary — and

24

finally he had left it behind altogether at the port in one of his periodic attempts to escape. Then the altar stone went — too dangerous to carry with him. He had no business to say Mass without it: he was probably liable to suspension, but penalties of the ecclesiastical kind began to seem unreal in a state where the only penalty was the civil one of death. The routine of his life like a dam was cracked and forgetfulness came dribbling in, wiping out this and that. Five years ago he had given way to despair — the unforgiveable sin — and he was going back now to the scene of his despair with a curious lightening of the heart. For he had got over his despair too. He was a bad priest, he knew it: they had a name for his kind — a whisky priest, but every failure dropped out of sight and mind: somewhere they accumulated in secret — the rubble of his failures. One day they would choke up, he supposed, altogether the source of grace. Until then he carried on, with spells of fear, weariness, with a shamefaced lightness of heart.

The first thing we notice is the catalogue of failures, or supposed failures; then the string of images suggesting disintegration and collapse: the "cracked dam," the "forgetfulness . . . dribbling in," the "rubble of his failures," "choke up the source of grace." One can scarcely help being struck by the sense of satisfaction, almost of complacency, with which the failures are paraded though in fact no priest on the run could possibly be expected to observe what are in the main matters of ecclesiastical discipline. This makes us suspicious. Are we really listening, we wonder, to the story of a hunted priest, a man who is subject to human weakness like the rest of us, but who nevertheless behaves heroically when he has to choose between apostasy and death? Or are we having a covert emotional appeal made to us by the use of a religious theme and setting? Are we simply listening to what is at bottom a somewhat melodramatic tale about a manhunt? I cannot help suspecting that this is the answer. My suspicions are confirmed by the language: the emotion-laden images and adjectives: *"cracked"* dam; *"rubble* of his failures"; the juggling with the words "despair," "unforgiveable sin," "surrender." This is not all. I think that under the pretext of using the "point of view" a highly personal, a distinctly unbalanced view of life, is being projected into a situation and a character with which it has very little to do.

Let us look at some more samples of the priest's unspoken thoughts:

> But at the centre of his own faith there always stood the convincing mystery — that we are made in God's image — God was the parent, but he was also the policeman, the criminal, the priest, the maniac and the judge. Something resembling God's image dangled from the gibbet or went into odd attitudes before the bullets in a prison yard or contorted itself like a camel in the attitude of sex. He would sit in the confessional and hear the complicated dirty ingenuities which God's image had thought out: and God's image shook now, up and down on the mule's back, with the yellow teeth sticking out over the lower lip, and God's image did its despairing act of rebellion with Maria in the hut among the rats.

I do not think that this time there can be any doubt. These are the novelist's reflections on life which are being put into the priest's mind. The novelist takes a very poor view of human nature. The passage begins with a formal reference to "the mystery at the centre of his faith . . . that we are made in God's image." But at once there is a sudden switch and a sudden descent: God's image is identified with an oddly assorted collection of individuals: the policeman at the top of the list, the judge at the bottom, the priest sandwiched in between the criminal and the maniac. The gibbet seems to contain an allusion to the Crucifixion and to the criminal being hanged; the "bullets" to martyred priests being shot. There is a violent contrast between them and the next presentation of God's image: "contorted like a camel in the attitude of sex." The way in which the dying movements of what we assume to be a martyr merge into the writhings of the fornicator illustrates very well what I said earlier of Greene's method of using the conjunction of religion and sex to heighten the emotional appeal of his work. For the sensational element lies in the reference to the Crucifixion and the triumphal entry into Jerusalem which are brought into close proximity with illicit sexual intercourse:

> Something resembling God's image dangled from the gibbet . . . or contorted itself like a camel in the attitude of sex.

> God's image shook now, up and down on the mule's back . . . and God's image did its despairing act of rebellion with Maria among the rats.

Greene seems here to be almost gloating over the disreputable behavior of human nature and there is something resembling a sneer in the repeated references of "God's image": "God's image" doing this or that, but whatever it is, it is nearly always discreditable: "the complicated dirty ingenuities which God's image had thought out" that inevitably provokes the response: "Wonder what they were?"

We should observe the tone in both passages. The highly charged vocabulary contrasts strangely with the lifelessness and lack of rhythm in the construction of the sentences, giving the impression in the first passage of something like a whine, and in the second of something approaching a sneer.

When the priest, seen from a distance by the dentist, finally crumples up before the firing squad, we are not filled with admiration for the simple man who in spite of everything died a heroic, a martyr's death. We feel that an enormous effort has been made to show that, in human terms at any rate, martyrdom is a thoroughly squalid affair, that the real saint, far from being like the one in the book the "churchy" mother reads to her children, is the man who departs as far as possible from the teaching of the Church, who is faithful in one thing only. He may have gone with Maria among the rats, but at least he didn't behave like Padre José.

The Heart of the Matter

The Heart of the Matter MIGHT FAIRLY BE DESCRIBED AS A companion piece to *The Power and the Glory,* but we shall see that in one respect at least it is notably inferior to the earlier novel. It deals like *The Power and the Glory* with an immature world, a world whose inhabitants are morally, mentally, and emotionally undeveloped. They are arranged broadly in three tiers: police, administrators, and natives who correspond to the police, expatriates, and natives in *The Power and the Glory.* Children play an important part, but in this novel they underline and prolong the immaturity of the adult world instead of providing a criticism of it as to some extent they do in *The*

Power and the Glory. What is more obvious in *The Heart of the Matter* than in almost any of the other novels is that Greene's world is a world of mediocrities. His protagonists are examples of what has been called, in another context, "the unheroic hero." They are never distinguished by their moral or intellectual qualities: the hallmark of the Greene hero is grievous moral weakness. The only two saints in his work appear to achieve sanctity by accident. The clergy are remarkable mainly for their inadequacy, which seems a reflection of the moral weakness of the laity. Their futility or their silence hastens the disaster; they arrive on the scene with empty words of comfort when it is too late and the protagonist is dead.

There is, as I have already suggested, the same sharp contrast in *The Heart of the Matter* and *The Power and the Glory* between the "inner" and the "outer" man, between the public and the private image, the office and its holder. The policeman's uniform confers an outward authority which is markedly at variance with the lack of inner authority of the individual. It also has the effect of concealing personal weakness from public view. The same is true of the civilian administrators whose position as state employees sometimes hides criminal tendencies. One is given premature retirement, another is transferred, for putting his hand into the till. A third commits suicide as the only escape from an intolerable situation created by his dishonesty.

Scobie, working as a police officer in an appalling backwater, has earned a reputation for integrity. He is known as "the Just": a local Aristides in the British bureaucracy who is respected alike by colleagues, friends, and the native population. The novel is largely devoted to an exposure of the man, to showing how undeserved the flattering title is. It is true that he is not scruffy or disreputable or given to the bottle or other men's beds. The source of his downfall is precisely what is esteemed a virtue by the secular world: his humanity, his feeling for his fellow human beings; in a word — a very terrible word in this novel — his "pity." It is a terrible word because virtue is turned inside out, because what is ordinarily a virtue becomes a fatal weakness. We are reminded here of the essential mediocrity of Greene's characters and of the "uncomfortable questioning critic" of his first novel. It is a sign of Scobie's immaturity and of his singular lack of insight into his own motives that he is taken in by his private cant about "pity":

> He had no sense of responsibility toward the beautiful and the graceful and the intelligent. They could find their own way. It was the face for which nobody would go out of his way, the face that would soon be used to rebuffs and indifference that demanded his allegiance. The word "pity" is used as loosely as the word "love", the terrible promiscuous passion which so few experienced.

The word occurs again in an account of Scobie watching his poor, silly, snobbish wife sleeping:

> He watched her through the muslin net. Her face had the yellow ivory tinge of atrabine: her hair which had once been the colour of bottled honey was dark and stringy with sweat. These were the times of ugliness when he loved her, when pity reached the intensity of a passion. It was pity that told him to go, he wouldn't have woken his worst enemy from sleep — leave alone Louise.

One would hardly feel inclined to describe either of these passages as distinguished prose, but their purpose is clear. Scobie's special pleading is really aimed at the reader. The comparison between the fortunate and the unfortunate, the use of a phrase like "terrible promiscuous passion," the pathetic account of Louise's ugliness, are intended to make us swallow the author's thesis about "pity." The faults in the writing are more pronounced in another passage in which Scobie reflects on his responsibilities towards his wife:

> He had always been prepared to accept the responsibility for his actions, and he had always been half aware too, from the time he made his terrible private vow, how far *this* action might carry him. Despair is the price one pays for setting oneself an impossible aim. It is, one is told, the unforgiveable sin, but it is the sin the corrupt or evil man never practices. He always has hope. He never reaches the freezing point of knowing absolute failure. Only the man of good will always carries in his heart the capacity for damnation.

There is a similarity between the tone and content of this passage and the passages I quoted from *The Power and the Glory*. It, too, is filled with special pleading and unconvincing arguments. The wicked man has a better chance of salvation than the man of good will who, we are told in a characteristically emotive phrase, has taken a "terrible private vow," which

29

after all is nothing more than to make an unprepossessing wife happy.

In *The Power and the Glory* we watch a movement which looks like a descent leading to martyrdom: in *The Heart of the Matter* we watch the descent of a man who seems, but only seems, to be betrayed by his good qualities and are left in doubt about his salvation. For if *The Power and the Glory* is one of the most popular of Greene's novels it is because there are genuine motives for the whisky priest's actions when he finds himself on the run in a hostile country. Scobie's "pity" is far less convincing. He is a very ordinary individual with the traditional public school virtues — decency, uprightness, kindness, integrity — who finds himself married to the wrong woman. He also has the characteristic public school vice: the sentimentality which underlies the heartiness and supposed manliness that are sedulously inculcated by the schools. In the supercharged atmosphere of a Greene novel the sentimentality produces disproportionate results because Scobie's sentimental pity for the underdog completely undermines his character, revealing the extreme brittleness of his virtues. He is guilty of one betrayal after another: his duty as a police officer, his loyalty to a faithful servant, his marriage vows, and finally his vows to the Church. A blubbering Portuguese captain is more than enough to make him betray his trust to his country and to do so without any serious struggle or apparently without any realization of the enormity of the offence. He is a believing Catholic, but simply in order to avoid paining his wife or arousing suspicion about his liaison with another woman, he makes a sacrilegious communion which could have been avoided without the slightest difficulty. Finally, he commits suicide on the pretext that it is the only way to avoid making two women unhappy, but in reality because he is too cowardly to face the situation created by his weakness — it would be too much for his "pity."

I have suggested that in one particular *The Heart of the Matter* compares unfavorably with *The Power and the Glory*. The superiority of *The Power and the Glory* lies primarily in the fact that the priest's simple faith does provide a point of reference, a positive standard which enables us to see the actions of the other characters in perspective. It is precisely this that is lacking in *The Heart of the Matter*. I have tried to show

30

that Scobie's "pity" is a sentimental illusion. What is more serious is that the illusion is bolstered up by an element of casuistry. It is suggested in one place that the Crucifixion was a form of suicide. This unorthodox suggestion becomes the excuse for Scobie's suicide which by implication is compared favorably with the suicide of the civil servant who could not face material difficulties which were more real than Scobie's sentimental difficulties. We hear much in the novel of corruption and decay, but the casuistry seems to me to point to something corrupt in the novel itself. For what we find in it is not so much an absence of moral perspective as a deliberate destruction of perspective in the interests of melodrama.

The truth is that sensational events like the sacrilegious communion and the suicide have no real motivation. The author set out to write a "theological thriller" about a Catholic gambling with his soul, which leaves us in doubt (as it was bound to) about the result of Scobie's "last throw." The protagonist is "rigged." What seems to have happened is that situation preceded character as it would in an adventure story. The result is that we have an incredible character used as an inadequate illustration of an impossible thesis.

The Later Novels

WE HAVE SEEN THAT IN THE RELIGIOUS NOVELS THE AUTHOR sets out to define a certain attitude towards belief. In his two most celebrated works it is the point of view of the weak man inside the Faith: in the later novels it is the point of view of the unbeliever or the man who has lost his faith. I think we must add that in two of them the criticism of religion is more drastic than anything in the works which preceded them.

On the first page of *The End of the Affair* we read:

> I hated Henry — I hated his wife Sarah too . . . So this is a record of hate far more than of love. . . .

These are the terms in which Bendrix, the novelist-narrator, speaks of his dead mistress and the man whose wife he stole.

The novelist takes a banal situation — two men and a woman — and gives it a peculiar twist. It is the end of a love affair, but a love affair in which there was more hate than love. For the word "hate" throbs, disconcertingly, all through the book:

> I would have liked to have left that past time alone, for as I write of 1939 I feel all my *hatred* returning. *Hatred* seems to operate the same glands as love. . . .

> That evening I was still full of my *hatred* and distrust when I reached Piccadilly. More than anything in the world I wanted to hurt Sarah. I wanted to take a woman back with me and lie with her upon the same bed in which I had made love to Sarah. . . .

Then there is the novelettish tone:

> There was no pursuit and no seduction. We left half the good steak on our plates and a third of the bottle of claret and came out into Maiden Lane with the same intention in both our minds. At exactly the same spot as before, by the doorway and the grill, we kissed. I said, "I'm in love".
> "Me too."
> "We can't go home".
> "No."

They don't. They have a go in one of those hotels in Paddington where

> you could get a room any time of the day for an hour or two . . . a real Edwardian room with a great gilt double bed and red velvet curtains and a full-length mirror.

There is a significant comment in Sarah's diary:

> Maurice's pain goes into his writing: you can hear the nerves twitch through his sentences.

It leaves us with the feeling that in this novel we have the projection of painful personal equations into imaginary characters. We must not attach too much importance to the miracles. It is a story of hate; the story of the most destructive emotion known to erring human nature. The author's intentions — his unconscious intentions — are summed up by the cremation of the saint at the end: the symbolical destruction of a loved-and-hated religion.

A Burnt-out Case was coldly received by some of Graham Greene's admirers on the ground that it lacks the "spontaneity" of its predecessors. It is the absence of the so-called "spontaneity" which commends it to me. If it is the best of the novels, it is because there appears to be a serious attempt to examine a situation without generating the overcharged atmosphere of *The Power and the Glory* or *The Heart of the Matter*. The theme is similar to that of the two earlier novels, but is stated much more explicitly in the dedicatory letter:

> This is not a *roman à clef,* but an attempt to give dramatic expression to various types of belief, half-belief and non-belief, in the kind of setting, removed from world-politics and household preoccupations, where such differences are felt acutely and find expression.

There are the missionary priests at the leproserie who are too busy with works of corporal mercy to have time to worry over the subtleties of moral theology — the only one who does comes near to losing his faith — or whether their strange guest goes to mass or not; Colin, the unbelieving doctor; Rycker, the spoiled priest; the natives all mixed up over God and the tribal god, Nzambi; and the stranger. A clue is provided by the blurb:

> A leper who is cured has sometimes gone first through the stage of mutilation — he is known as a "burnt-out case."

There is clearly an intellectual thesis here: that there is a parallel between the physical states through which some lepers pass and the mental states of some men. The missionaries think, in so far as they leave themselves time to think, that Querry is a believer who is going through a period of aridity. He puts it differently with an amusing salaciousness which is characteristic of his creator.

> I'm no genius, Rycker. I am a man who had a certain talent, not a very great talent, and I have come to the end of it. There was nothing new I could do. I could only repeat myself. So I gave up. It's as simple as that. Just as I have given up women. After all, there are only thirty-two ways of driving a nail into a hole.

It is one of the virtues of the book that the situation, or the state of the protagonist, is a simple one: there are no dubious moral conflicts and no melodrama. Interest is maintained — the adventure story again — by the fact that we do not know the answer. The priests and the "churchy" Rycker interpret Querry's state of mind in one way; he himself does so in quite another. There is the "big moment" when he is suspected, quite wrongly, of adultery with the "babydoll" Mme Rycker and shot dead by her husband in a drunken fury. And we are left wondering whether he was in fact on the verge of conversion: we are not left in any doubt about his superiority over all the other representatives of the different kinds of belief and half-belief excepting only the unbelieving Dr. Colin.

The originality of the novel lies in the creation of a new concept. For the "burnt-out case" ranks with the "hunted man" and the "outsider" of other novels and of other novelists. It appears to be as much an author-projection as they and its implications are disturbing.

At the opening of *The Comedians,* Graham Greene's latest novel, a small oddly assorted group of people of various nationalities find themselves on board a Dutch boat with a Greek name bound for Haiti. The novel describes their adventures and misadventures ·on that island. Greene's Haiti is not, like the Congo of *A Burnt-out Case,* a "region of the mind." What he offers among other things is a realistic picture of a country under dictatorship: a petty dictatorship no doubt, but none the less horrifying for that:

> Haiti was not an exception in a sane world: it was a small slice of everyday taken at random.

The story is related in the first person. The narrator's name is Brown. He is the son — probably the illegitimate son — of a vamp, was born in Monte Carlo and educated by the Jesuits. They thought that he might have a vocation for the priesthood. They were wrong. He was expelled from the school for gambling at the casino: the prank was discovered when someone saw him drop a five-franc roulette-token into the collection in chapel. He had never known his father. His mother, always behind with the school bills, had already abandoned him and he had to live by his wits. A chance post card took him to Haiti where his mother had acquired, through the timely death in a car crash of a wealthy lover, an hotel which he inherited when she herself died of heart failure while in bed with a Negro lover many years her junior. The hotel prospered until the advent of the dictatorship drove the tourists away. Brown has failed to sell his hotel in New York and is on his way back to a place which for all its horrors is the nearest he has known to a home. He becomes involved in the resistance, not out of bravery or conviction, but in an attempt to rid himself of a man whom he believes, wrongly, to be his rival in the affections of his mistress. He is obliged to seek refuge in St. Domingo. His love affair with the German wife of the Uruguayan ambassador to Haiti peters out when the ambassador is transferred to another post, possibly because he granted asylum in his embassy to Brown's "rival" at Brown's request. His hotel has been seized by the Haitian government and in order to earn a living he becomes, not altogether inappropriately, a partner in an undertaker's business.

"Brown is not Greene," writes the author in a dedicatory letter. Perhaps not, but they have a number of traits in common. Brown has lost his faith, or thinks he has, but the voice we hear in this pronouncement on the variety of beliefs is surely the voice of the sophisticated novelist and not that of a rootless individual who has been living on his wits:

> I had a sense of coloured balls flying in the air, a different colour for every faith — or even lack of faith. There was an existentialist ball, a logical-positivist ball. . . .

He shares his creator's immense admiration for Henry James — hardly an author likely to appeal to a confidence man — as well as his taste for the salacious joke. When they are in bed together, his mistress says to him:

> "Perhaps you are a *prêtre manqué*."
> "Me? You are laughing at me. Put your hand here. This has no theology."

The title explains the theme. It is a variation on the theme of the "inner" and the "outer" man: the contrast between the French *être* and *paraître,* between what a man *is* and what he *appears* to be. For all the characters are playing parts in life and from time to time realize that they are.

This is the narrator on his role:

> Life was a comedy, not the tragedy for which I had been prepared, and it seemed to me that we were all, on this boat . . . driven by an authoritative practical joker towards the extreme point of comedy.

35

I am sure that the chargé [d'affaires] would have disapproved of my cuckolding a member of the diplomatic corps. The act belonged too closely to the theatre of farce.

This is the cuckolded ambassador:

"We mustn't complain too much of being comedians — it's an honourable profession. If only we could be good ones the world might gain at least a sense of style. We have failed — that's all. We are bad comedians, we aren't bad men."

Finally, the mistress:

"You should have been a novelist", she said, "then we would all have been your characters. We couldn't say to you we are not like that at all, we couldn't answer back. Darling, don't you see you are inventing us."

He does indeed "invent" his mistress. He is afflicted by the same insensate jealousy as the narrator in *The End of the Affair*. This contributes to the collapse of the affair but is not, as we shall see, the root cause.

Greene uses the word "comedian" in its literal English sense, meaning a comic actor or an actor playing a role in a comedy, but in the course of the novel its meaning is considerably extended. Some of the characters begin by playing comic roles and end by finding themselves involved in tragedy. Jones, the fake who boasts of non-existent experiences of jungle warfare and claims a military rank which was never his, appears to be a comic figure, but underneath there is an element of decency which takes him into the resistance where he loses his life. Mr. Smith, who polled 10,000 votes against Truman in the presidential election on a vegetarian ticket and has come to start the movement in one of the most unlikely of countries, begins equally as a figure of fun. We are meant to laugh when we see him swimming in the hotel pool where the ex-Minister of Welfare (to whom he had an introduction) has been driven to suicide:

There in the pool, avoiding the gardener's rake, swam Mr. Smith, wearing a pair of dark grey nylon bathing pants which billowed out behind him, giving him the huge hindquarters of some prehistoric beast. He swam slowly up and down, using the breast stroke and grunting rhythmically. . . .

36

He seems to be a figure of fun because of his proverbial American innocence, and he dismisses all accounts of the horrors of the dictatorship until they are forced upon his attention. But he is, for all his foibles and absurdities, a man of real integrity, and once he realizes the situation his integrity imposes itself, creates a standard by which the other characters and the dictator's minions are judged.

If the word "comedian" is used in its literal English sense, it is also used in the sense commonly given in France to the word *comédien* in the seventeenth century when it meant an actor who was a member of a theatrical company and took part alike in comedy or tragedy. It is here that the parallel with the "inner" and the "outer" man is most evident. All the characters are playing parts in life which have either been thrust upon them by circumstance or have been devised by themselves to conceal their real selves. Brown not only resembles Bendrix in *The End of the Affair*: he has affinities with Querry, the "burnt-out case." His "rootlessness" recalls Querry's peculiar form of disillusioned lethargy. He says of the end of his affair:

> Neither of us would ever die for love. We would grieve and separate and find another. We belonged to the world of comedy and not tragedy.

Again:

> The rootless have experienced, like the others, the temptation of sharing the security of a religious creed or a political faith and for some reason we have turned the temptation down.

"Rootlessness" is seen to be another variety of the unbelief or half-belief studied in earlier novels. The real man, always supposing that there is a real or inner man, has been effectively stifled by the comic role. For the indifferent man can only play a comic and not a tragic part.

The book is written with the author's customary skill. The setting is admirably done; the performers in what should perhaps be called a tragi-comedy are finely observed and the style has the sobriety of *A Burnt-out Case*. But in the nature of things a study of indifference must make less impact on the reader than the study of a man who had known violent passions which had burnt themselves out.

37

The Playwright

THE DEARTH OF GREAT DRAMA IN EUROPE FROM THE BEGINNING of the nineteenth to the middle of the twentieth century is one of the unexplained mysteries of literary history. With the exception of Russia and two of the Scandinavian countries no European country produced a dramatist who can indubitably be described as "great." I myself am unable to propose a solution, but the view that the decline of the drama was due almost entirely to the rise of the novel strikes me as too much of a simplification. There is no reason why the same writer should not excel as the author of plays and prose fiction as Marivaux, Heinrich von Kleist, and Chekhov all did. What is perhaps more to the point is that novelists like Henry James, Mauriac, and Greene have felt the urge — eloquently described by Greene in the preface to *Three Plays* — to abandon the arduous one-man job in the study, to see their creations come to life on the stage in a way they never can on the printed page, to rub shoulders with producers and actors, to attend rehearsals and tailor their scripts to fit the new medium.

Greene is the author of four plays which have enjoyed professional production in Britain and the United States. *The Living Room* was the first of the four and it seems to me to be the best, but none of them is of the caliber of the most successful of the novels and none adds anything of importance to what is known as the author's "message."

In *The Living Room* two elderly spinsters, Teresa and Helen Browne, are living with their brother James — a priest who lost both legs in a motor accident twenty years ago and is unable to exercise his priestly function — in a large rambling house in north London. Although a conventionally pious Catholic, Helen, the younger of the two sisters, is terrified of death. She has persuaded her brother and sister that any room in which a member of the family dies shall be disused and closed. This means that the family's living space has been gradually shrinking, leaving only one room in which they can "live" together.

The play begins with the arrival from the provinces of their twenty-year-old niece, Rose Pemberton. Her mother has just died and she is an orphan. Although a demure girl she celebrated the funeral night by opening her legs to Michael Dennis, a forty-five-year-old university lecturer in psychology and a non-Catholic who had been a favorite pupil of Rose's non-Catholic father. He is also a married man. The theme of the play is really a study in inadequacy: the different ways in which the relatives are inadequate to help a Christian girl caught in a dilemma which because of the religious element is more than the ordinary dilemma of a man and two women. The uncharitable Aunt Helen prattles about mortal sin, sends a servant to spy on the girl when she goes to the Regent Hotel for an afternoon's copulation with her lover, and claims to have kept her in the Church because she foiled her plan to run away with him. Aunt Teresa is more tolerant and more understanding, but is bullied by her sister. The priest — his leglessness is presumably a rather cruel symbol of the inadequacy he shares with nearly all Greene's clergy — speaks with two voices. When he speaks as Uncle James he is kind, sensible and understanding; when he speaks as Father Browne he falls into the pious platitudes which swamp the counsels of Uncle James and eventually drive Rose to despair:

> "Dear, there's always the Mass. It's there to help. Your Rosary, you've got a Rosary haven't you? Perhaps Our Lady . . . prayer."

There are other favorite Greene topics — the disappointing nature of the encounters at the Regal Hotel:

> "Uncle, it isn't wonderful at all. It's sad, sad."

If the faith of the family is unable to help, the lover's knowledge of psychology is equally useless.

Michael's hysterical wife appears. Rose is moved to a "pity" which proves as disastrous as Scobie's. She realizes, when she sees husband and wife together, that marriage means something more than bed, that even when a man expresses his readiness to leave his wife there is often a bond which is not easily broken. In a frenzy the hapless girl commits suicide by taking an overdose of the sleeping tablets brought by the wife to

39

blackmail husband and mistress and inadvertently left behind. The spell hanging over the house is somehow broken by Aunt Teresa's decision to turn "the living room" where Rose died into her bedroom.

Greene has reservations about his next play. He tells us, in his preface, that *The Potting Shed* was constructed out of a discarded and unfinished novel, and that he takes no pleasure in it except for the first act. It is the only one of the four plays that I have not seen on the stage, but when I read it I found it one of the most entertaining. Good straight Catholic stuff! An old rationalist, long since forgotten by the world, lies dying. The family prevent his son James from seeing his dying father. He is the black sheep for reasons which the family will not disclose and which the psychoanalyst friend is unable to discover. Little by little it transpires that the old rationalist's brother was converted and is now a whisky-sodden priest who has lost his faith, but continues after a fashion to perform his function. Years before the family had kicked up a fuss because he was instructing his youthful nephew James. Instead of becoming a Catholic, James had hanged himself in the potting shed and been found dead by the gardener. Uncle William prayed and offered his faith for his nephew. God accepted the wager. James was miraculously brought back to life and the uncle lost his faith. The old rationalist, it seems, was a "fraud" because he believed in the miracle and never withdrew his rationalist tracts. His wife, who disbelieved in the miracle, protected him by keeping up appearances. James has been tormented all his life because he knows that there is some mystery connected with the potting shed, but has never been able to find out what it was. All ends happily with the uncle regaining his faith, the nephew presumably on the threshold of conversion and about to remarry his divorced wife (their marriage had been wrecked because his complex about "the potting shed" prevented him from putting up much of a show in bed).

Greene compares *The Complaisant Lover* to an "entertainment." It is an amusing comedy with, apparently, "no religious interest." A middle-aged dentist's wife falls in love with a secondhand bookseller and there are fun and games at an hotel in Amsterdam. The lover alerts the husband by an anonymous

40

letter in the hope that he will divorce his wife. He doesn't. They agree that the lady shall remain with her husband who will raise no objection to a discreet affair with the bookseller.

The author speaks of the manic-depressive side of his nature and remarks that in spite of his enjoyment in writing the play, he discovered that on reaching the final curtain the "depressive" mood had contributed almost as much as the "manic." There is an element of "black comedy" in the ending: there is plenty of wit and shrewd observation of people in the play as a whole.

Carving a Statue is by far the least successful of the four plays. When it was produced in London in the autumn of 1964 it was poorly received by the critics and ran for only six weeks with steadily shrinking audiences. It is a study of a middle-aged and not very talented religious sculptor — denomination unstated, presumed Roman Catholic — who for fifteen years has been working on a gigantic statue of God the Father. In spite of the author's disclaimers the play obviously drips with symbolism, but the only things that interested me were the seduction and attempted seductions. When the hopelessly neurotic solicitor in John Osborne's *Inadmissible Evidence* asks his women staff, on the intercom, how their sex-life is doing or makes the pair of them on the office floor after closing time, the effect is merely fatuous. It is far otherwise with Catholic writers. For one has to admit that when it comes to a seduction the popish writers really are unbeatable, perhaps because they are less inhibited, or simply more immodest, than their unbelieving *confrères*. In *Carving a Statue* a brassy little tart in skin-tight jeans sets to work on the sculptor's teenage son, trying to steer a reluctant hand to that part of her anatomy where it should repose during a really good kiss. She fails. The sculptor, a widower, re-enters and the son departs. In a religious art studio there is naturally much talk of "virgins," a term which sorely puzzles the innocent son. "I think you're still partly a virgin," remarks the father to the little piece. "I'd better finish the job." He carries her off to a small office in a corner of the studio. A few minutes later the lady emerges minus the jeans and asking the way to the bathroom. The sculptor thinks that it will help him to put the finishing touches on God's left eye — the one with the malicious squint. The boy reappears with a new girl friend

41

who is deaf and dumb and chaste. It is now the turn of the family doctor — a rare old goat — who tries his wiles on her in the consulting room. She makes a bolt for the street and is killed by a passing car. There is a reconciliation between father and son on the scaffolding surrounding the immense white elephant. No doubt it has some deep religious meaning, but once again I didn't get it.

The Dilemma of the Christian Writer

GRAHAM GREENE, FRANÇOIS MAURIAC, AND JEAN CAYROL have all declared at different times that they are Catholics who write novels and not Catholic novelists, or that they are simply novelists who have written books in which some of the characters happen to be Catholics. Our first reaction is that this attitude is mistaken. We know that the statements were prompted to some extent by the novelists' fear that they might be suspected of bias or turning out works of edification or that the "churchy," shocked by their preoccupation with violence, sex and sin, might make trouble with the bishops. Nobody wants them to indulge in pious platitudes, shirk the harsh realities of the contemporary world or, for that matter, spoil the view with too many fig leaves. We do, however, expect a man's religion to be the center of his writing, to be the unifying principle which provides an objective scheme of values that will enable him to place all experience in perspective. If Christian writers seem to fail, if instead of "seeing life steadily and seeing it whole," their work sometimes appears violent and unbalanced, we must try to understand the reasons. The distinction they seek to draw and the books they write are symptomatic of our time; they are conditioned by historical changes and are highly significant. What we are concerned with is the dilemma of the Christian writer in the Age of Angst.

A truly Christian literature in which experience is assessed calmly in the light of eternal values can only be produced by a society which generally speaking is Christian. This, of course, does not mean that everyone in it is leading an exemplary

Christian life. It means that the writer is a member of a community which accepts the Christian faith even if individuals do not always practice it, that his work is the reflection of a communal outlook even if he is not dealing with a specifically Christian subject, that his conception of the nature of man is basically Christian.

I sometimes find it difficult to think of Chaucer either as a Catholic poet or as a Catholic who wrote poetry. Yet in spite of his bawdiness and the gorgeous Wife of Bathe's plea for "octogamye" — she is actually quite a good theologian — he was plainly both. He is also a characteristic representative of the virtues of medieval literature. I think we can say that the value of medieval poetry, the value of Dante or Chaucer or Langland, different as they are in outlook and stature, lies to a very considerable degree in the feeling of stability and confidence, in the belief in a fixed unchanging order, a world with a heaven above and a hell below, which it succeeds in communicating to the reader.

In the sixteenth century there is a break in the pattern. The community is divided into a large number of warring factions with conflicting outlooks. The Church is replaced by the churches; Theology by the theologies; Philosophy by the philosophies; Science by the sciences. The literature like the art of the period is dominated by a feeling of unrest, by the writer's and the artist's sense of living in an age of crisis. The change, indeed, is more immediately evident in its art than in its literature. In a medieval work like the carvings at Chartres the emphasis falls on two themes: Creation and Incarnation. The men who made them could not omit all references to the sorrowful mysteries, but they are confined to a glimpse of the foot of the Cross and a couple of Nails on one of the porticoes. It is only with the Age of Baroque that the Crucifixion becomes the center of religious art, that poetry and painting drip with the Blood of Christ and the martyrs, that sculptors are continually representing the saints writhing in ecstasy.

It was the origin of that imbalance which is the keynote of modern literature and art as stability was in the middle ages. What the Age of Baroque tried to do was to absorb and transform the discoveries about the natural world — the new insights — which were the fruits of the Renaissance. It was, for all its brilliance, a form of compromise and the beginning of a losing battle. What happened was something very different. Instead of religion transforming alien elements, it has been dominated, almost swamped by them. And the process has been going on with gathering momentum for four hundred years.

We can say that in the middle ages religion was the principle of unity, but that it has now become the disruptive element. Instead of being the bond between the individual Christian and the community, it is religion which separates him from his fellows and turns him into an alien figure. Instead of the strength which comes from being the member of a community, he belongs to a shrinking minority at odds with the rest of the world. This accounts for what I have called the quality of the religion in the religious novel. Dogmas do not change, but the religious ethos and the emphasis given to particular dogmas are undoubtedly colored by the age. The sense that he belongs to a minority, that Christian faith is only one of a vast number of conflicting philosophies, that he has to fight to give it adequate expression accounts in a large measure for the violence and the tension which are characteristic of modern Christian writers as they are of modern Christian artists like Rouault and Graham Sutherland. It also accounts not merely for the emphasis on the sorrowful mysteries, but for the tremendous preoccupation with sin. We might go on to say that in the past religion imposed the pattern and shaped the man. Today it no longer does so with the same decisiveness as before; it is to a great extent shaped by man's emotions. Instead of the pattern being formed by the impersonal, the enduring, the normal, it is too often shaped by the personal, the fortuitous, the abnormal, until in the end religion itself is in danger of becoming a single factor in a private world of hatred, lust, and guilt.

The effects are perhaps most apparent in the damage done to the image of man: the concept of human nature.

> What a piece of work is Man! [says Hamlet]. How noble in reason! How infinite in faculty! in form, in moving, how express and admirable! in action how like an angel! in apprehension how like a god; the beauty of the world! the paragon of animals!

"Ni ange ni bête," said Pascal more soberly. This was the Christian conception of man. He belonged partly to the spiritual and partly to the animal worlds. He was imperfect, but was endowed with reason. He was engaged in a constant struggle to control his animal instincts and preserve a state of equilibrium, or to transcend his animal instincts and advance in the way of perfection. Above all, he was endowed with an immortal soul and was capable of salvation.

According to one critic, the pessimistic approach of Pascal himself and of the free-thinking La Rochefoucauld was responsible for what he calls "the demolition of the hero." Once the hero was gone, a great deal followed. In the nineteenth century the realists and naturalists, who based their novels on the philosophy of determinism, reduced man to what Balzac called a "temperament" and Zola an "appetite." The short answer to Pascal is contained in the three words of the title of one of Zola's novels: "la bête humaine." Pascal's "angel" has been eliminated from the equation.

At the beginning of the present century there was a strong reaction against materialism which was seen to be an impoverishment of human nature — we remember Virginia Woolf's famous attack on the "materialism" of Bennett, Galsworthy and Wells — and in the twenties there was a great deal of talk about the emergence of the "new man." The antidote turned out to be a poor one. The characters of E. M. Forster and Virginia Woolf herself are civilized, intelligent, and sensitive, but they have no souls. Man is thrown back on personal relationships — one of the magic phrases of the twenties — personal feelings, personal standards of integrity only to find that they are perpetually letting him down. Feelings do, indeed, become used up, worn out, as surely as in Greene's "burnt-out case," but in these writers who have no vision of salvation, there is nothing left except to have the victim cremated and scatter the ashes.

D. H. Lawrence made a prodigious effort, proposing a sort of earthly salvation by gigantic copulation. The result appears in his own verdict on the protagonist in *The Rainbow*: he had come, we are told, to a "stability of nullification." In Sartre man becomes an anxiety-ridden neurotic fretting about freedom and "bad faith." His plight is still worse in Samuel Beckett with his miserable tramps waiting for the god who will never turn up, or the blind tyrant and legless imbeciles immured in dustbins in *Endgame*. For the "endgame" is also the end of man.

Whatever the writer's philosophy, man appears in modern literature as an isolated individual racked by tension and doubt. Sometimes he suffers in solitude and silence. Sometimes he is a fugitive from society; the "outsider" in rebellion against smugness and complacency which drives him first into sin, then into crime. For the sinner in Greene and Mauriac is the counterpart in the order of Grace of the "outsider" of a Stendhal, who invented him, or a Camus, in the order of nature. At other times the lonely, frustrated individual escapes breakdown and loses himself and his identity by plunging into the masses, joins the cohorts of workers and becomes a cog in the party machine, or simply degenerates into one of the herd of rutting animals which fill the works of Henry Miller.

These, then, are the factors which determine the quality of the religion in the work of Graham Greene. It would be wrong to close our eyes to its shortcomings and unfair not to try to understand the reasons for them, or to withhold our gratitude for what he and other contemporary Christian writers have done for us. For whatever his shortcomings or his limitations, in this world the Christian novelist has one lesson of immense importance to teach us all. He does remind us on every page that human beings, however vilely they behave, have immortal souls; that the alternatives salvation-damnation are the greatest reality, indeed the only reality, in the world.

SELECTED BIBLIOGRAPHY

I. WORKS BY GRAHAM GREENE

Except where the contrary is stated all books by Graham Greene were first published in London by William Heinemann, Ltd.

Novels

The Man Within	1929
The Name of Action	1930
Rumour at Nightfall	1931
It's a Battlefield	1934
England Made Me	1935
Brighton Rock	1938
The Power and the Glory	1940
The Heart of the Matter	1948
The End of the Affair	1951
The Quiet American	1955
A Burnt-out Case	1961
The Comedians (Bodley Head)	1966

Entertainments

Stamboul Train	1932
A Gun for Sale	1936
The Confidential Agent	1939
The Ministry of Fear	1943
The Third Man and *The Fallen Idol*	1950
Loser Takes All	1955
Our Man in Havana	1958

Short Stories

The Bear Fell Free (Grayson & Grayson)	1935
The Basement Room (Cresset Press)	1935
Nineteen Stories	1947
Twenty-one Stories	1954
A Sense of Reality (Bodley Head)	1963

Plays

The Living Room	1953
The Potting Shed	1958
The Complaisant Lover	1959
(Collected as *Three Plays*, Mercury Books, 1961)	
Carving a Statue	1964

Travel

Journey without Maps	1936
The Lawless Roads	1939
In Search of a Character	1961

Essays and Criticism

British Dramatists (Collins)	1942
The Lost Childhood (Eyre & Spottiswoode)	1951

Children's Books

The Little Train (Parrish)	1947
The Little Fire Engine (Parrish)	1950
The Little Horse Bus (Parrish)	1952
The Little Steam Roller (Parrish)	1953

Poetry

Babbling April, Oxford: Blackwell	1925

Miscellaneous

Why do I Write?
(with Elizabeth Bowen and V. S. Pritchett)
    London: Percival Marshall   1948
The Spy's Bedside Book (Ed. with Hugh Greene)
    London: Hart-Davis   1957

II. ON GRAHAM GREENE

Allott, Kenneth, and Farris, Miriam, *The Art of Graham Greene.* London: Hamish Hamilton, 1951.

Atkins, John: *Graham Greene.* London: Calder, 1957.

Gregor, Ian, and Nicholas, Brian: *The Moral and the Story.* London: Faber, 1962 (Graham Greene, pp. 186-216).

Lees, F. N.: 'Graham Greene: a Comment', *Scrutiny,* Vol. XIX, No. 1. October, 1952, pp. 31-42.

Madaule, Jacques: *Graham Greene.* Paris: Editions du Temps Présent, 1949.

Martin, Graham: 'Novelists of Three Decades', pp. 394-414 of *The Pelican Guide to English Literature: 7 The Modern Age.* London: 1961.

Mesnet, Marie-Béatrice: *Graham Greene and the heart of the matter.* London: Cresset Press, 1954.

O'Brien, Conor Cruise: *Maria Cross.* Imaginative Patterns in a Group of Catholic Writers. New ed. London: Burns & Oates, 1963. ('Graham Greene: the anatomy of Pity', pp. 57-84. This book was originally published under the pseudonym of Donat O'Donnell by Chatto & Windus in 1954.)

Pange, Victor de: *Graham Greene* (Classiques du XXè Siècle). Paris: Editions Universitaires, 1953.

Pryce-Jones, David: *Graham Greene* (Writers and Critics). London: Oliver & Boyd, 1963.

Rischik, J.: *Graham Greene und sein Werk* (Schweizer Anglistische Arbeiten: Band 28). Berne: Verlag A. Francke, 1951.

Traversi, Derek: 'Graham Greene' in *The Twentieth Century,* Vol. CXLIX, Nos. 889 and 890. March and April, 1951, pp. 231-40, 318-28.

Wyndham, Francis: *Graham Greene.* London: Longmans, 1962.

Zabel, Morton Dauwen: 'Graham Greene', pp. 287-93 of *Forms of Modern Fiction,* ed. W. van O'Connor. Minneapolis: University of Minnesota Press; London: Geoffrey Cumberlege, 1948.